STALKING SALMON & WRESTLING DRUNKS

STALKING SALMON

WRESTLING DRUNKS

Confessions of a Charter Boat Skipper

PETER L. GORDON

HARBOUR
PUBLISHING

Harbour Publishing Co. Ltd.
P.O. Box 219, Madeira Park, BC, V0N 2H0
www.harbourpublishing.com

Maps by Roger Handling
Edited by Arlene Prunkl
Copyedited by Brianna Cerkiewicz
Cover design by Diane Robertson
Text design and diagrams by Shed Simas
Printed in Canada on paper certified by the Forest Stewardship Council®

Harbour Publishing acknowledges the support of the Canada Council
for the Arts, which last year invested $157 million to bring the arts to
Canadians throughout the country. We also gratefully acknowledge
financial support from the Government of Canada through the
Canada Book Fund and from the Province of British Columbia
through the BC Arts Council and the Book Publishing Tax Credit.

Cataloguing data available from Library and Archives Canada
ISBN 978-1-55017-743-5 (paper)   ISBN 978-1-55017-744-2 (ebook)

With a twinkle in my eye, this book is dedicated to the important people in my life: to my dad and mum, and to Christine, Alan, Ian, Anna, Debbie, Martin and Laurie Gorilla.

An extra note of thanks to Christine for all her encouragement and help.

Table of Contents

South Vancouver Island

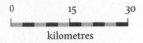

0   15   30
kilometres

VANCOUVER ISLAND

Strait of Georgia

Oak Bay

Canada
USA

Pacific Ocean

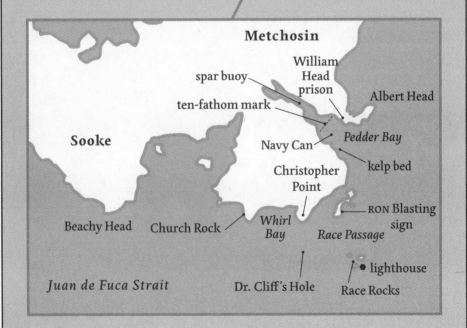

Metchosin

spar buoy

William
Head
prison

Albert Head

ten-fathom mark

Sooke

Navy Can

Pedder Bay

kelp bed

Christopher
Point

RON Blasting
sign

Beachy Head   Church Rock

*Whirl
Bay*

Race Passage

Juan de Fuca Strait   Dr. Cliff's Hole

● lighthouse

Race Rocks

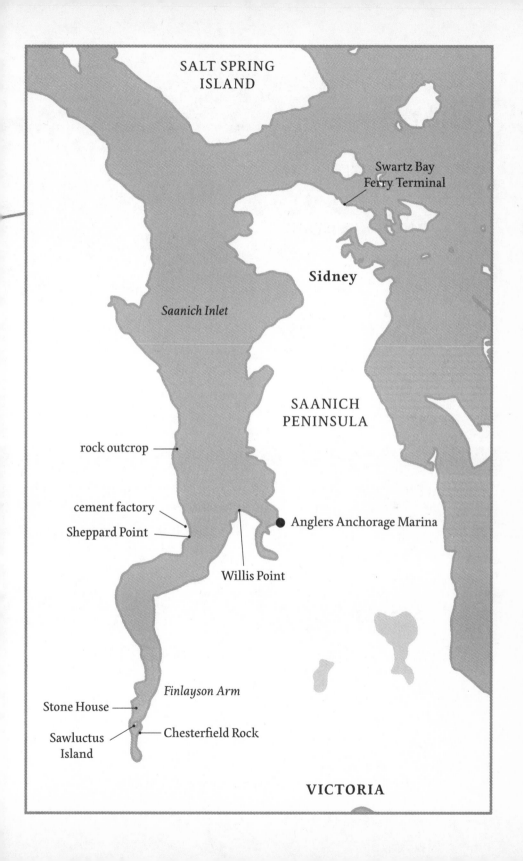

SALT SPRING
ISLAND

Swartz Bay
Ferry Terminal

Sidney

Saanich Inlet

SAANICH
PENINSULA

rock outcrop

cement factory

Sheppard Point

● Anglers Anchorage Marina

Willis Point

Finlayson Arm

Stone House

Sawluctus
Island

Chesterfield Rock

VICTORIA

"It is in truth not for glory, nor riches, nor honours that we are fighting, but for freedom alone, which no honest man gives up but with life itself."

—Declaration of Arbroath, Scotland, April 6, 1320

Introduction

For a twelve-year period from 1978 to 1990, I ran a charter fish-ing boat on the West Coast of Canada, off the shores of Vancouver Island. It is a time in my life that instills delight whenever I flick through the ship's log and photo album. The stories and anecdotes in this book are all taken from that log and from my personal memories and those of my children, who have vivid recollections of their time aboard my charter boat, a fifty-foot Monk cruiser named MV *Kalua*. Revisiting these experiences has been incredibly gratifying and entertaining as we laughed togeth-er at the memories.

This is not a manual on how to fish, although fishing is the thread that binds the stories together. This book is not so much about fishing as it is about human nature and people's quirks and eccentricities and, in some cases, their enormous generosity of spirit. Some of my charters were marvellous, almost magical. Mixed in with those joyful charters were some that still move me to great sadness, while others were peopled with arrogant fools who could spoil a quiet sunrise with their presence. The biggest pleasures of my charter fishing business happened when my trin-ity came together—great weather, great people and great fishing.

xiv   STALKING SALMON & WRESTLING DRUNKS

I formed Magna Charters Ltd. in Victoria, BC, Canada, both to give me a means of financial support during the summer months and to allow me the freedom to teach drama for the Bastion Theatre during the off-season. In Victoria the charter boat season runs from late May to a few weeks after Labour Day. There is some trickle business beyond that date, but it is referred to as "shoulder" business and consists of only enough activity to cover a little more than operating expenses.

I chose salmon fishing as a means of financial support over numerous other possibilities because the sea, rivers and lakes have always been my safe place. It is difficult to explain the peace in my heart as I drifted slowly past Race Rocks with a crew of like-minded people, observing the plunging birds and the wondrous orcas and the majestic Olympic Mountains and . . . smelling the sea lions. The scent of the sea lions is a bonus and not appreciated by all comers. More observations on this unique smell can be found in the second chapter of this book.

When I folded Magna Charters in 1990, I felt it had run its course and served its purpose. The decline in the salmon stock in my areas was one of the reasons. It was still possible to go out and catch some salmon but it was more difficult. It was time for a change, so I purchased a fifty-acre equestrian centre near Duncan on Vancouver Island and used it to raise ostriches . . . but that is another story.

For privacy, I have taken the precaution of changing the names of everyone mentioned in this book except those of my family.

chapter 1
Visitors from Texas

"Well, we have a tall Texan."

A hundred yards from our slip, by the marina office, I could see our party making its way down the rattling metal ramp to the floating dock. Between them they were carrying enough bags and baskets for a ten-day fishing trip.

"So what's your guess?" I asked Sten.

This was a game Sten and I played before each charter. Simply by the appearance of our guests, we would guess at how the charter was going to turn out. I counted the number in the party—I knew there were supposed to be five.

"They're all there," I said. "So what do you think?"

We knew from the booking that a local resident was hosting visitors from Texas whom he wanted to take salmon fishing. We also knew they wanted to troll as opposed to drift fish. In those days, trolling—fishing with the vessel in motion—entailed the use of large flashers, hand-cranked downriggers, heavy rods with heavy line. By far my favourite choice was drift fishing—allowing the vessel to gently drift with the current with the engine off.

Sten was peering at the advancing group through my Zeiss binoculars. "They're going to be a pain," he predicted. "I'll take the

1

helm the whole trip. You handle them." Usually the man at the helm had little to do with the guests. His job was to find the fish, keep us clear of kelp and keep us off the rocks.

"I don't think so," I said. "I'm not hearing that little alarm bell in my head that I sometimes get with certain idiots. So go ahead— take the helm. I think this is going to be a blast."

I said this partly to tease him but also to initiate the bet. We invariably had a bet on what the people were going to be like. This time I was certain I was right, but the bet was on as usual.

It was a lovely, clear day with no wind. We would reach the high slack tide—slack tides are prime fishing periods—in about an hour and a half. If the people were pleasant and the fishing was good, except for the fact that I'd rather be drift fishing, the trip would be perfect.

Sten, my assistant deckhand, was a retired commercial fisherman in his mid-thirties when he applied for a job to work on my boat. From the age of fourteen he had worked as a deckhand on commercial fishing boats during his summer vacations. He had fished the waters all the way to the northern tip of Vancouver Island and beyond. He knew more about fishing than almost anyone in my circle of friends. Like me, he preferred to fish for salmon with light tackle. Trolling using forty-pound test line and rods that resembled broom handles gave us much less joy, but sometimes we had to pull out the trolling gear and put it to use because the customers requested it.

Sten had retired from commercial fishing after being caught once too often by a fierce storm off the northwest coast of Vancouver Island. It was a killer storm lasting five days; much of that time Sten was lashed into his bunk, severely seasick. After the storm subsided, half the deck gear was torn away and every pane of glass in the wheelhouse was shattered. The skipper, who was also Sten's uncle, refitted his boat then put it up for sale along with its licence. That was when Sten applied for work with me.

In addition to his quiet good nature and enthusiasm, Sten was a magical fisherman who never lost his joy of fishing and loved to see other people catch fish. Big fish—he loved it when they caught big fish. A fish, to Sten, was always a salmon. Even a 150-pound halibut was simply a slab, not a fish. Moreover, he didn't drink or use drugs, his language was sanitized and he was always on time—and he could cook. His reaction to our advancing party from Texas was out of character for him, so much so that I briefly doubted my intuition. I took the binoculars from Sten's hands and watched the group as they made the long trek down the dock to our slip at the farthest point from the marina office.

No, I thought as I watched them approach, *they seem all right to me*. But I would let Sten have his way. He could handle the helm for the entire trip while I dealt with the guests and the gear.

This was my ninth year operating the company. Several things had changed over the years, including the introduction of a saltwater fishing licence along with serious catch quotas. In my first year of running the operation, saltwater licences did not exist and almost any size of salmon could be kept. The old-timers use to fill their freezers with coho grilse, immature salmon that had to measure only six inches to be allowed to be kept. Those they did not cook during the year would be ploughed into their compost heaps before the cycle would start all over again. Nearly a decade later, that practice had largely come to an end. There was also a move away from the food-catching mentality to a sport-fishing mentality. This new approach had become so well entrenched by my ninth year that many of the sport fishermen were releasing their undamaged catch for the purpose of conservation. We applauded these changes.

By my third year of operation, I had shifted our charters from a strict focus on catching salmon to a salmon-fishing trip with overtones of a nature tour. During the off-season I encouraged Sten to read and study various nature books so he could identify and learn about the birds in our region, their habitats and their life cycles. Other books taught him about the wildlife below our keel and the struggle for life that played out with each changing tide. He was clever and a fast learner, so it wasn't long before he was giving lectures at the stern of the boat on the life cycle of Steller sea lions or some other form of wildlife visible from our deck. Occasionally—not often—he would mix up his facts. He once described the life cycle of a puffin when instead he meant a cormorant—two very different birds. However, none of our guests appeared to notice these mistakes, and I was never sure whether Sten was doing it on purpose. To be on the safe side, I would make a point of correcting him after the charter, but only when we were alone, sitting in the galley having a cup of coffee and discussing the events of the day.

In this relaxed atmosphere, I would also make notes in the ship's log concerning the fishing conditions, the type and number of salmon we caught, the lures we used and the depth at which we caught our fish. Memorable charters when the people, the weather and the fishing were perfect required additional space in the log. It is these recorded memories that have served as the basis for this narrative.

Sten turned on the blower to remove potentially explosive gases from the bilge and then he fired up the engine. The VHF radio clicked on, followed by the CB, which immediately began to chatter like a parrot on an illegal stimulant. Sten turned it down and adjusted the revs on the engine. This was all done just as our party arrived alongside and prepared to board.

"Permission to come aboard, Skipper?" the local fellow asked. I liked this little ceremony.

"Please make yourselves at home. The *Kalua* welcomes you," I said. *Good start*, I thought as I glanced at Sten at the helm.

My vessel was called MV *Kalua*, a name and spelling I inherited and at first wanted to change. But the very idea was considered such bad luck that when I tried to change it, no one would answer my calls on the CB. So that plan quickly sunk like a stone in Victoria Harbour.

The first person to come aboard was the local man, who introduced himself as Jake. This was perplexing, since during the entire trip no one else called him Jake except me, and it remains a mystery to this day. He clamped me by the shoulders and whispered in my ear that his guests were special friends from Texas and he really wanted them to catch a salmon. I told him we would do our best.

Next the tall Texan, Chuck, came on board. Reaching over the railing, he helped a diminutive blond woman onto the deck, who turned out to be his wife. Scarcely more than five feet tall, she was wearing skin-tight, neon blue designer jeans with red embroidery on the back pockets, matching deck shoes and a light blue blouse with three-quarter-length sleeves. A light scent hung about her that reminded me of lavender.

"Are you wearing hand cream?" I asked. Most fishermen agree that a lure should not carry human or chemical smells. Women often came on our charters wearing hand cream, which tainted the lures with the odour of the cream. The hands of smokers had the same effect, so we would try to convince them to wash their hands as well.

"Yes," she said. "Do you like it?"

I looked at her closely for the first time and realized she was a stunningly beautiful woman. "Remember to wash your hands before you handle the gear."

She looked up at her husband with slight embarrassment as though expecting a reprimand. "Don't say it!"

"Honey, it ain't nothing." He flashed her a generous smile. They had obviously discussed the use of hand cream before leaving home.

The rest of the party clambered on board, struggling with hampers, bags and baskets. I helped them down the companionway and into the forward cabin, where they could stow their gear and make themselves at home while we cast off.

With Sten at the helm, I did the honours. I unfastened the spring lines, which prevent fore and aft surging, then the bowline. There was no wind so I gave the bow a push away from the dock while Sten slipped the engine into reverse and spun the helm a half turn. The *Kalua* slowly moved in reverse and strained against the stern line I had wrapped around a bollard on the dock. As the bow swung around, I fed out the line until the vessel had spun a full 180 degrees and was facing the channel that would take us into the bay. With Sten's eyes on me, I nodded at him when the boat was in position, unwrapped the rest of the stern line from the bollard and stepped onto the stern deck with the line in my hand. We smiled at each other. The slack wind had helped us to execute a flawless cast-off, but no one would notice except us.

During the next half hour I made sure everyone had their licences and that they were properly completed. I also went through the routine of demonstrating how to flush the toilet in the head—the W.C. Although I'd made many upgrades to the boat, the toilet was still operated manually with instructions attached to the back of the head door. At least twice a week one of our guests would emerge from the head with a bewildered look and ask for help with flushing. It was simple: use the toilet, lower the lid, put your right foot on the only pedal available and work the lever back and forth to pump the bowl clean. Easy, but more complicated than pushing a handle, and baffling to many members of the general public.

While I checked fishing licences, poured cups of coffee and pulled hot Danishes from the oven, Sten took us at planing speed to our first fishing spot. As we approached, he throttled the engine back slowly, and the boat settled from its plane into the water. Sten turned on the paper sounder—also known as a depth sounder or echo sounder—and I heard the *click*, *click*, *click* of the stylus scoring the thermal paper. In five minutes Sten would call out that we were ready to begin fishing. Before going to the stern deck to set up the fishing gear, I'd have a quick look at the paper sounder, which would show us the baitfish; this in turn would give me an idea of the depth at which to start fishing. Sounders were originally developed to show depth; revealing the presence of fish turned out to be a bonus. The downriggers were already in place and the lead weights ready to be mounted onto their stainless steel cables.

The routine of setting out the fishing gear always attracted a crowd on our spacious stern deck. First I set up the downriggers, then the rods with the lures at the end of their lines. On this day I wanted a slow roll to our bait, meaning the lure imitates a wounded spiralling herring. Sten throttled back as I lowered the gear to fishing depth. And just like that, we were in business.

With everything set and in place, I turned back to the group of fishermen and explained that when a salmon took the bait, the bell on the arm of the downrigger would ring and the fish's strike would release the line from the downrigger. I would pick up the rod and crank in the slack line until I felt contact with the salmon on the end, then hand the rod to the first designated fisherman.

"Have you decided who's going to take the first strike?" The group of eyes was staring at me intently, but I directed my question to Jake.

"I think that should be Chuck," he said tapping the tall Texan on the arm. *Not a surprising choice*, I thought.

"Aw, come on, Al, you take the first strike. You're local—show us how to lose a fish."

Al? Jake? Okay, whatever. I laughed along with everyone else. "Show them how it's done, Jake," I said. "You're not going to let some Texas greenhorn jerk your chain, are you?"

As I spoke Sten's hand shot up; simultaneously the portside downrigger bell gave a single ring. Out of habit I snatched the rod out of its holder, cranking furiously on the handle until I felt the heavy weight of the fish at the other end. Sten had put the engine into neutral and come down to help me. I held the rod tip up and tightened the drag slightly. I could feel the fish thrashing at the end of the line but not running.

Sten raised both downriggers and unclipped the weights. "Any size?" he asked.

"Under twenty pounds, over fifteen."

"You going to hand it off?"

"Uh-huh." I knew what he meant with his question. We would have a better chance of landing the fish if I played it. Returning to port with a fish on ice is important for the overall experience. Still, I knew Jake and Chuck would be eager. I called over my shoulder, "So who's it going to be?"

Jake was standing beside me, trying to say something. I grabbed his right arm and placed the rod firmly into his grip. "You play it," I said. "It's a good fish."

As I handed him the rod, the fish took its first run. When a fish "sounds," it is heading for the bottom of the ocean. This salmon didn't sound—it didn't head for deep water—but screamed to the surface in a headlong rush for the horizon, trailing line behind it.

"How much line do you have on this thing?" Jake asked under his breath. I could tell his adrenalin was pumping by the quiver in his voice and his jerky movements.

"Enough. Keep your rod tip up and keep pressure on the fish."

His rod tip came up twenty degrees and he stopped reeling as the fish peeled out line, pulling against the drag on the reel.

"Watch out," I said. "It's going to stop and thrash, so keep pressure on it." Before Jake could follow my instructions, the salmon sounded then came streaming back at the boat.

"Reel!" I shouted. "Come on, reel faster or it'll throw the hook. If that happens, I'll throw you overboard." My joke didn't go over too well. Jake was quivering and barely able to turn the reel handle in a circle. We called these fishermen square shooters because they turned the handle in a jerky manner instead of a smooth circular movement.

"Faster," I said in his ear. "Come on, catch up to him."

He was reeling frantically now, picking up the loose line. At the moment he caught up to the fish, his rod doubled over and was nearly yanked out of his hands. The entire length of the rod was jerked up and down forcefully as the salmon thrashed underwater in a desperate battle to save its life. The reel again began to creak out some line.

"Drop your rod tip and reel as you do, pull up slowly, then drop your rod tip and repeat the action. It's a pumping action," I told him.

For the next fifteen minutes, the salmon fought for its life while Jake struggled to bring it alongside. Each time the fish saw the boat it screamed out line, which had to be retrieved with some effort. Each time it took a run it was shorter; exhaustion was setting in and no amount of courageous instinct could match the sophisticated reel and line we were using.

The smooth, stainless steel ball bearings in the reel rotated flawlessly as the monofilament line stretched instead of snapping and the rod acted as a shock absorber, reducing the thrashing of the salmon to manageable bounces at the end of the rod. A brief but courageous final run and the salmon turned on its side. I netted it and swung it onto the deck. It was gasping, its gill flaps working to extract oxygen from the air.

The boat erupted in cheers and Chuck gave a loud "Yee-ha!" Looking at the salmon, I knew that even if I could persuade the fishermen to return this beautiful, rainbow-silver fish to the ocean, it would die. The effort of the struggle and the shock of being caught were too much.

I reached for the Priest and banged the fish on the head. "Go home now," I said softly—a ritual that was an act of respect for the life we had just taken. A "priest" is a small club used for ending a fish's life. They are sold in stores but I made mine. The name comes from the idea of administering last rites to the fish, or perhaps from stories of priests beating the tar out of young boys who were the unfortunate targets of their disciplinary measures. I still have the Priest from my charter boat.

Jake was quivering.

I shook his hand, saying, "You played that well."

"No," he said. "I couldn't have done it without you."

"Don't be silly. I just cussed in your ear a bit."

"Do you think it will go twenty pounds? It has to be at least twenty! I've never caught a twenty—fourteen is my biggest."

"This time next year it'll be at least thirty," I said, knowing how fishing tales became taller with the passage of time. "But right now—before time, stories and too much fresh air put weight on it—I would guess it's seventeen." I looked up at Sten, who was at the helm studying the paper sounder. "What do you say, Sten? Seventeen?"

"Eighteen at least—right now." He smiled.

I pulled out my trusty scales and read off the weight: "Eighteen!"

Again there was a cheer from the crowd on the boat. Everyone shook hands while I picked the salmon out of the green mesh of the landing net and placed it in the cleaning tray at the stern of the boat.

"How do you want it?" I called out. "Ears on or off?" No one answered. They were congratulating one another and opening chilled cans of beer. We were still drifting in neutral; Sten was still at the helm examining the paper sounder.

Leaving the fish in the tray, I made my way through the group of people, up the four steps to the helm and over to the sounder to look at the readings.

"Nice haystack," I said, referring to the haystack shape the stylus scored on the sounder paper. It represented the outline of a school of herring. At the base of the haystack were white areas where the herring had been chased by feeding fish or birds. *Probably salmon*, I thought. "What do you think, Sten?"

"I think we should do an about-face and make the same run."

I smiled. "Let's do it. But give me time to clean the fish. Nice fish," I added.

"They're all nice," he said. "Especially the big ones. I'll cruise us back at three or four knots."

"Fine. Let me know if we pick up any top hats." A top hat was our term for a fish that showed on the paper sounder as a large circumflex accent. It indicated a large salmon. Since we both spoke French, which uses that accent frequently, it was an obvious way of describing the mark on the paper. When I returned to the cleaning tray, both Chuck and Jake were holding cans of beer and staring at the salmon in the tray. "Ears on or ears off?" I asked Jake.

"Ears on," he said with a smile. "They look prettier that way." "Ears on" means the fish is eviscerated, its gills removed as well as any lice clinging to the vent area. The head and pectoral fins are left on, which makes the fish look as though it has been mounted.

Chuck was watching with a wry expression. "Damn," he said. "Back in Texas we use fish that size for bait."

"Damn," I echoed back at him. "You don't have any salmon in Texas."

We all laughed. Chuck and Jake smiled at each other and had a sip of beer. It was all good-natured. Chuck was playing on his image as a Texan, and the fact that he was at least six foot six and wore a grubby and mashed-up ten-gallon hat added to the stereotype.

"Seriously," Chuck said, "are you telling me this is what you guys call a fish?"

There was a crinkling around his eyes and he winked at Jake so I knew the remarks were meant for me. I also knew I was in for a protracted leg pulling. It was all right—it was their charter and he was a guest. "Maybe the next one will look like a fish to you," I said.

"It'll have to be able to swallow this one," he retorted.

This is turning into lots of fun, I thought.

I cleaned the fish using our stainless steel knife, which had a large yellow handle and a spoon attached to it with electrical tape. I unzipped the fish from vent to chin before cutting out the vent, leaving it attached to the rest of the intestines. When I separated the intestines from the salmon with a neat cut to the throat, out came a handful of guts in one clean package. I cut out the gills followed by the kidney, which was scooped from the base of the spine using the spoon attached to the knife handle. Next, to see what it had been eating, I cut open the stomach, which was packed with herring the size of those we were using at the end of our flasher. I threw the handful of guts over the stern railing to a small flock of seagulls that had started to follow us as soon as the fish was in the cleaning tray.

Good start, I thought. *The first one's always the hardest to catch.*

By the time I had the fish ready to stow in the chest with crushed ice, we had cruised quietly back to our starting point and turned into the flooding tide. I washed my hands in a bucket of salt water, dried them and prepared to reset the lines. One of Jake's friends, a foggy-looking fellow who introduced himself as Mason and was wearing clothes that were obviously too small for him, asked if he could help set the gear.

"Have you ever set lines using a downrigger?" I asked.

When he said he had not, I suggested he stand back and watch how it was done. He looked so disappointed that I changed my mind and talked him through the procedure, which added an extra ten minutes to the line set. I let him do everything except attach the line to the downrigger, a procedure that is an acquired skill. Too much pressure and the fish is unable to disengage the line from the downrigger cable; too little pressure and it will pop free with the slightest change of current.

After we'd set the downriggers, I asked, "Who takes the next strike?"

A general conversation broke out, everyone suggesting someone else when each person really wanted to be next.

This wasn't getting us anywhere so I stepped in. "The local resident is going home with a salmon, so now we have to send our guests away with a one. Chuck, that means you or your missus. Who is it to be?"

"Blue Eyes," Chuck said to his wife, "I'd like you to be next."

Sometimes we didn't learn guests' names until we were setting lines later in the charter. I wasn't about to call her Blue Eyes, and she avoided any awkwardness by saying, "Please call me Jeannie. Mrs. Jeanne Arnold, the recent Mrs. Jeanne Arnold."

Her speech was very Southern, softer than Chuck's but just as nasal.

"Congratulations," I said, a bit surprised. "Does this mean you two are newlyweds on your honeymoon?"

Chuck stepped from behind her and draped his arm over her shoulder. She took his hand and held it in both of hers.

She's so short and he's so tall, I thought. They were radiating love. Their pleasure splashed onto everyone in the group, and I found myself grinning along with everyone else.

"We've been married just four days," Chuck said. They continued beaming at each other in such a happy, transparent manner that it was infectious. I reached out to Chuck and shook his oversized hand. I could feel it was a hand that had done some practical labour, and I wondered if he had a ranch and rode horses. Instead of shaking Jeannie's hand I gave her a hug, which brought a round of applause from everyone. It had all been so spontaneous I felt a bit silly.

"So are you going to be next, Jeannie?"

She looked up at Chuck with real pleading in her eyes. "I don't think I can, honey," she said, "I mean, Albert had a tough time with his fish and it wasn't even so big. I don't think I could hold onto the rod." She looked anxious and Chuck seemed unsure of what to do.

I didn't want to get into a discussion about an eighteen-pound salmon being small. Instead I said, "How about if we run the same routine we did with the last one? I'll pick the rod out of the holder and strike the fish. If I think it's over ten pounds, I'll hand it to Chuck, and if I think it's under ten, I'll hand it to Jeannie. Does that sound okay?"

Some mumbling and murmuring ensued as they all looked at one another and tried to decide what to say. Finally, Jake agreed with a nod of his head. "Okay, let's do it that way."

I glanced up at Sten but he was staring ahead, so I made my way up the companionway to the helm and had a look at the paper sounder. There was lots of feed and we were on the edge of a large haystack that started at around two fathoms and went down to six. Six feet to a fathom meant thirty-six feet to the bottom of the haystack. Salmon usually lurk just below the feed.

"I'm going to drop the starboard line down to sixty feet," I said.

"Good idea." He kept his eyes focused ahead.

"Anything up front?"

"Kelp."

"Much?"

"Enough."

"Let me know if it's going to be a problem."

"No problem yet."

I went to the stern of the boat and checked the tension on the reels. It is important to have the drag set tight enough to set the hook when the fish strikes, but not so tight that the fish cannot run. A light breeze was blowing and I could smell the herring and the kelp in the air. When the ocean has an abundance of feed, the air around you starts to smell of fish oil. While it is not a strong smell, there's nothing better to make a fisherman feel optimistic. Kelp, with its smell of iodine, is always welcome.

Sten was moving the boat forward slowly on a zigzag course, partly to avoid the islands of kelp floating toward us on the flood tide, and partly to alter the movement of the bait and flashers at the end of the downriggers. When kelp is around it's important to check your lines frequently to be sure you are not trailing some of it from your lure.

For the next while I worked the lines. The whirl of the downriggers became commonplace to the guests, who had spread throughout the boat and no longer stood around as I brought up the lines to inspect the bait.

As noon approached, Jake and his friends busied themselves unpacking their hampers of food and setting it out on the table in the galley. The smell of the food imposed itself on the fresh sea air, so I kept my distance and stayed as close to the stern as I could. Something about some picnic foods and the aroma of damp, limp sandwiches can turn my stomach, especially if tomatoes are involved. Sten, on the other hand, kept peering expectantly down the companionway into the galley like a wolf in search of a carcass.

The sounder was still showing dense feed so I altered the depth of the lines a few times to see whether that would draw a strike. It didn't. I decided to change the bait from the fresh herring we were using to a Tomic plug—but only on the port-side downrigger. I had a favourite beaten-up plug that often produced a fish when little else was working. I brought up the downrigger and swung the weight into the cleaning trough before unsnapping the flasher with the bait attached to it, then replaced it with my plug using an eighteen-inch leader. After lowering the weight back into the water, I watched the action of the plug for a few minutes, trying to understand why this plug worked so well. I had no idea—it seemed like all the other plugs I had in my tackle drawer. I put the line down to forty-eight feet. I wanted these people to go home with memories of catching a slug—a really big fish, the kind you might lie about—off the West Coast of Canada.

We fished through the flood tide and into the slack. The activity was good, with the bell on the downrigger continually ringing and giving everyone a chance to play a fish. By the time the tide began to turn we had five salmon on ice. We had lost as many.

Chuck and Jeannie caught a brace of salmon between them. Sten and I had both been wrong. Despite her delicate, polished appearance and her initial trepidation, Jeannie surprised me by playing her fish with easy skill, which made me realize there was depth to this young bride. She also had a sense of humour. While they didn't break world records, they had some good fish that had fought with courage. Just before the tide started to run I suggested we pull up all our lines, find a quiet spot and finish our lunch. Everyone agreed, so Sten cruised us to a serene eddy we often used, cut the engine and came down to the galley to plough down some food. I was surprised to see him mingle with the guests since he had been adamant about remaining apart from them, but I kept my thoughts to myself. I'd remind him later that I'd won our bet.

At the stern of the boat I kept an eye on our drift; although we were in a back eddy, the tide was changing and currents could shift abruptly. *This is perfect*, I thought. There was just a slight breeze, the sky was a crackling blue, the Olympic Range was crystal clear from twenty-two miles away and the rumble of the changing tide was just beginning to build.

And I have a nice bunch of people. These are the good old days.

At the start of the day, I had been concerned Chuck was going to be a loudmouth who ruined the fishing for everyone; instead he'd turned out to be a thoughtful fellow with a fine sense of humour. Of course, he couldn't let an occasion go by without pulling our legs about how much bigger and better everything was in his home state of Texas. I'd guessed him to be a rancher, but during one of our conversations he told me he owned a string of fast-food franchises—over thirty of them, Jake later told me. I did the math and realized that Chuck was in a financial comfort zone enjoyed by very few. To his credit he had done it all on his own, starting with one franchise he could barely afford to purchase and sleeping and eating in the back room. Here he was, nearly twenty years later, living the good life. How can you complain about one man's well-earned success?

"What are you thinking, Skipper?" Chuck had come up behind me.

"I was thinking it's about time we caught you a real Canadian salmon."

"I don't think you've got any real fish up here. If you ever come down to Texas, give me a call and I'll take you out to catch some real fish." There was humour in his voice and laughter in his eyes. He looked around and took a deep breath. "But it sure smells good up here, and it's sure pretty."

We stood quietly, soaking in the scenery and feeling the boat gently shift in the current. Without warning, an orca breached twenty feet from the stern of the boat. Behind it, a second orca propelled its glistening black and white body into the air, landing its massive nine-ton hulk on its side and seriously rocking the boat.

Chuck was thrown back, and as he braced himself against the bulkhead, I saw real fear in his eyes. "What the hell is that?" he yelled.

Without hesitating, I shouted back, "Canadian salmon!"

chapter 2
A Man of Grace

The first time Cliff fished with us, he was in a mixed group of guests aboard our newly refurbished *Kalua*. His sister, Alison, had made the booking based on a glowing recommendation from her friends. When she called, the only questions she asked were the time of departure and whether her brother should pack a lunch to bring with him.

Subsequently, for four consecutive years, Cliff booked at least one charter with us each summer. During that time we became good friends and he became our fishing legend. I write this with a smile because I know if he were to read these words, he would punch me in the shoulder. One of his charms was that he never took himself seriously. However, he was the consummate example of how, in life, it is important to be in the right place at the right time with the right set of skills. From our point of view, he was our man.

On his first charter, Cliff—Dr. Cliff McGee—was booked with three other people. In the group was a single fellow called Rae who was togged out in camouflage pants and shirt. He had no interest in fishing; his interest was photography. During the charter Rae spent a great deal of time at the bow of the boat with his cameras and bag, taking pictures of anything that stirred him. With his own Thermos of tea and a packet of sandwiches, he was quite content to enjoy the ride. At the end of the charter he left a fat tip for Sten and thanked us both vociferously for a marvellous experience. I never saw him again, but later that year I received a large brown envelope containing an article he had written for a national magazine that included some of the pictures he had taken while he was out with us.

The two other guests on this charter were US naval officers from a war vessel moored in Esquimalt. They introduced themselves as Ricardo and Jensen. While Rae, our photographer, and Cliff, our doctor, wore idiosyncratic clothing, these two looked as though they had picked their clothes out of someone else's locker. There was not a hint of navy apparel in their selection. They both wore jackets and shirts better suited for portly men and pants turned up at the cuff. They explained that their shipmates had hidden their clothes as a practical joke and what they were wearing had been scrounged from more sympathetic colleagues. They certainly added an interesting element to the group.

On our way out to Race Rocks, a marine ecological reserve in the Juan de Fuca Strait, I asked everyone how they would like to fish. To a man they wanted to troll, so I told them how we rotated strikes and asked them to work out who was to be first up. We would run two lines. The tide change would happen in about an hour and a half, but I expected to land some fish before then. It was a lovely cruise out to the rocks with such an animated, optimistic group.

We saw an osprey returning to its nest carrying a grilse in its talons, and the Steller sea lions were on full display lounging on the rocks surrounding the lighthouse at Race Rocks. But they stank—there was no polite word for it. The reek of their digested fish diet was so strong it made your eyes water. In the summer months, under the right wind conditions, the smell could force you to leave the area. On this particular day, the sky was overcast with a threat of showers. Fortunately the wind was not blowing in our direction, so the smell was negligible. I had spent some time in Vietnam, and the smell reminded me of a sauce they make in that gorgeous country with anchovies and salt. In North America it is sold as fish sauce; in Vietnam it is called *nuoc man*.

We cruised through Race Passage up to Church Rock, where Sten turned us around to face the ebbing tide and I set the lines. Ricardo, the youngest of the naval officers, had drawn first strike so I ran him through the strike procedure. Within twenty minutes we had our first hit and our first fish in the boat. It was a beautiful eight-pound coho, sparkling clean, free of sea lice. While pictures were being taken, I reset the lines and changed places with Sten.

He kept the lines at the same depth. Within ten minutes we had another fish on. Cliff was supposed to take the second strike, but he insisted Jensen take it. It turned out to be another splendid coho about the same weight as the first. In the fish trough they looked like twins; they were obviously from the same run. While Sten dressed the fish and stowed them in the ice chest, I cruised back to Church Rock and turned us back into the ebbing tide. The paper sounder showed vast layers of baitfish going down ten fathoms.

The squawking of seagulls, diving on the surface into shoals of baitfish, obscured all other sounds. At the helm I could barely hear the *click, click, click* of the paper sounder. I moved us farther out so we could fish the edges of the bait and avoid some of the messy debris the feeding gulls were dropping.

Before Sten lowered the lines of the downriggers, I had him change the heavy trolling rods for spinning gear with single-action reels holding fifteen-pound test line. The mood on the boat was lighthearted; it was a joy to be in a group of men who loved the scenery, the camaraderie and the fishing. Cliff and the officers were exchanging life stories and showing pictures of their wives and children. They found common ground in places they had lived and even thought they might have friends in common. Cliff kept refusing to take a strike, insisting the young naval officers have the fun. There was so much laughter at the stern of the boat that Rae joined them for a while and took pictures of the fishing activity. He didn't say much, just kept repeating, "This is great, this is just great," as he took a series of pictures with the sophisticated collection of cameras hanging from his neck.

Almost on schedule, the ebbing tide went slack. I made a long, slow loop and headed straight toward Church Rock. Twenty feet before we would have run aground, I spun the wheel hard to starboard. The effect was to drop the trolling gear into a hot spot right in front of Church Rock. Sometimes this manoeuvre produces a twenty pounder. But not on this occasion, so while we kept trolling toward Race Passage, Sten and I changed places. Between the two naval officers we had five fish on ice. I thought it was time we brought in a slug, something Cliff could show off to his sister.

I brought up the portside rod and attached a five-inch silver and bronze spoon to the line before lowering it to forty-five feet. This particular spoon revolved and jerked from side to side, imitating a wounded herring in escape mode. Sten, watching me intently, knew exactly what I was doing. Slowly he altered our course so we would pass directly over a sweet spot just before we entered Race Passage. As we approached the spot, I watched Sten and he watched the paper sounder. Still watching the sounder, he raised his right arm. I lowered the downrigger, with the spoon attached to it, down to sixty-four feet.

Given our speed, the tide conditions and the drag on the downrigger cable, I hoped I had placed the spoon directly into a deep channel. When Sten's arm came down I raised the downrigger, which brought up the spoon. Before I could look away from the gauge on the downrigger, the bell rang. I jerked the rod out of its holder and reeled furiously to catch up to the fish. At the same time, Sten threw the boat into neutral and was at my side cranking in the second downrigger.

"Any size?"

I didn't answer—I was concentrating on reeling as quickly as I could. The fish had taken the spoon and was racing for the surface. Before I could make contact it breached cleanly out of the ocean, snapping its head back and forth, trying to throw the lure. Then it sounded, and that was when I caught up to it. The speed with which the line was running out let us know it was a fish with authority.

I turned to find Cliff standing beside me. "You ready?" I asked.

He held out his right hand and I placed the rod into his grip. The line was peeling out, throwing a light spray.

"You've got fresh fifteen-pound test," I said. "The drag control is in the middle of the spool."

"I've got a reel just like it, only for fresh water."

"Great. Just keep your rod tip up and keep pressure on the fish."

While the fish continued to run, Sten unclipped the weights from the downriggers and put them in their box, then removed the downriggers and the rod holders from their brackets. The deck was clear. Cliff had lots of elbow room. This, we knew, was what we had come for.

Each time I stuck into a nice fish and handed off the rod, I had mixed feelings. While I knew I was running a business and customers were paying for the fishing experience, it was hard to hand off a rod with a strong salmon at the other end when the person taking the rod clearly had no clue about how to play it. Watching Cliff was different. I could see he was experienced and skilled simply by the way he anticipated the fish and held the rod.

I looked up at Sten, who nodded at me.

I nodded back. "What do you figure?"

"Thirty."

"That's my guess."

Cliff played the salmon with a lighter drag than I would have suggested. Two or three times the fish sounded before spinning around and shooting to the surface. Gripping his rod as the line whirled out of the reel, Cliff cranked maniacally on the handle to bring in the slack line as the fish charged back to the surface. It was an uneven battle. The gear we were using and the skill of the fisherman was overwhelming the heavy salmon. Its only hope was to throw the hook, but Cliff stayed in firm contact with it and let his rod wear it out. After he'd played the fish for twenty minutes, I brought out a director's chair and walked Cliff backward into its seat. He was a cool customer, but I could see his knees rattling together. Of course, while he played the fish the two high-spirited officers and Sten kept volunteering to take the rod. They told him they didn't want him to tire and were only thinking of his well-being. They even promised to hand the rod back to him when he asked for it. He was having none of their hijinks; instead he just smiled and told them in terse, naval language to catch their own fish.

During our charters, we used a rough estimate to gauge the length of time it would take to net a salmon. When using spinning gear the estimate is a minute per pound, although I once netted a twenty-seven pounder after only two minutes. But that is another story.

After sounding half a dozen times, the fish was about twenty feet directly below our stern, thrashing frantically. Without

prompting, Cliff began pumping the fish to the surface, alternately reeling then dropping the rod tip so it touched the water
before pulling it up to raise the salmon. When it saw our propeller it took a short run, but the steam was out of it. Without any
further struggle, Cliff was able to reel in the last ten feet of line
and steer the fish into the landing net.

Sten took over. Snapping the handle up and effectively
locking the fish into the basket of the net, he swung the fish
onto the deck. He looked at his watch. "Thirty-two minutes,"
he said aloud.

During these activities, Rae had migrated from the bow to
the stern where he recorded the event with his cameras. The two
officers clapped wildly and slapped Cliff on the back. I shook his
hand and gave him a hug and joined in the shouting and hoot-
ing. We all couldn't have been more pleased that he had landed
his fish. He couldn't keep a smile off his face. In a flash, I saw
the ghost of a twenty-five-year-old Cliff standing on the deck,
balanced on the balls of his feet and exuding the confidence of
youth. The white hair was gone, as were the white moustache
and prescription sunglasses. They were replaced with a sleek
pair of Polaroid glasses, and his hair was a rich brown and his
skin uncreased.

In the next instant, the vision was gone and the old Cliff was
again before me. He stared as if entranced at the glistening chinook that was still in the folds of the net. "Damn, that's a pretty
fish. It's almost a shame. Do you think it will go over twenty-five?"

After the Priest had done its job, I handed my trusted scales
to Sten. "Better weigh it before it starts to put on weight."

With the hook of the scales under the salmon's chin, Sten
lifted it off the deck. "Thirty-one on the nose." There was another
round of applause while Sten put the fish in the tray.

"Cliff, do you have a camera?" Rae asked.

"In my bag—it's on the seat in the galley." Without a word Sten fetched the bag and gave it to Cliff, who pulled a simple camera from a side pocket and handed it to Rae. "Will you take a picture?"

Rae took the camera and had a quick look at it. "Is it automatic?"

"Point and shoot."

"Got it. Stand in the corner and hold up the monster." With a bit of a struggle, Cliff lifted his salmon out of the trough and took a couple of steps back. He held it chest high while Rae took some pictures. The camera whirred and clicked loudly enough for everyone to hear.

"Thank you," Cliff said. "This will prove to the fellows back home that I really caught a nice one." He turned to Sten with dancing eyes and a barely suppressed smile on his face. "Did you say it's thirty-five?"

Without missing a beat, Sten replied, "At least." The whole crew broke into laughter and clapped again.

Cliff fished with us for four subsequent summers, and his legendary status aboard the *Kalua* only grew because of his charming character and magical good luck. The second summer he booked with us, he had with him the picture of his thirty-one pounder from the previous year. He announced that he wanted its twin. The guests who were sharing his charter chimed in and said they too wanted a fish that size. Sten and I rolled our eyes. They made salmon fishing seem like a trip to the supermarket.

Well, here comes the spooky part. We cruised out to a can-shaped buoy just past the lighthouse and picked up some nice fish in the eight- to twelve-pound range—delicious dinner fish. They were respectable but certainly not thirty pounders. For a while we stopped fishing, cruising around to admire the lighthouse and drifting quietly while the guests had their lunch. After lunch, we fired up the engine and I put out two downrigger lines. Cliff had already regaled everyone with an improved version of his catch from the previous season. In his account, it had taken "an easy forty-five minutes to land my thirty-eight pounder using twelve-pound test line and a trout rod." Sten and I enjoyed the story but winked at each other. We had the ship's log as a witness to the real event.

With the downriggers in place and the lines attached to them, we began to troll through Race Passage. Sten was at the wheel. I recall looking up at him and realizing he was going to take us over the identical spot where Cliff hooked his thirty-one pounder the previous year. On Sten's signal I lowered a line into the hot spot and again on his signal, I pulled the line up. Just like magic, the bell on the downrigger shook twice; then the line was free. I snapped up the rod, reeled in the slack line and handed the rod to Cliff, who was already standing beside me. The events were nearly a carbon copy of the previous year. This time Cliff did not need to sit down—his legs still rattled but he had more control. Just like the previous year, everyone pulled his leg while he played his fish. Also like the previous year, the salmon was successfully brought to the net and tipped the scales at thirty pounds.

This scenario repeated itself the third and fourth seasons he booked with us. The sweet spot where we picked up these thirty pounders became known to us as Dr. Cliff's Hole. In the ship's photo album were pictures of his thirty pounders. He would joke that we should pay him to fish with us, an idea I often turned over in my mind when the fishing was slow and the guests were grouchy. Perhaps in an effort not to jinx it, we never took any other guests to that special spot.

Cliff's fifth booking happened in an odd way. Sten and I took out an early-morning charter with poor results. We cast off at 3:30 AM and fished the change of tide. The group, though enthusiastic and boisterous, had been poor fishermen. They managed to lose every fish we handed off to them. Sten and I were sure that one of the fish was over twenty pounds. When I presented the bill for the charter to the host of the party, she complained that it had been an expensive "boat ride." I reminded her they had played but lost five salmon.

"What difference does it make if we're going home without any fish?" she moaned.

Under these circumstances, I usually kept my own council. In this case, unfortunately, I failed to follow my own advice. "Hmm," I said. "Maybe you could stop at a supermarket on your way home if you want to be sure of having a salmon to take with you."

Immediately I regretted my sarcasm. Needless to say, this remark further soured the trip, so after they had disembarked and we had cleaned up the boat, I sent Sten home for some much-needed time with his darling.

After he left, I pulled out the ship's log and filled it in. I went through the maintenance records and decided that one of our fuel tanks was low and needed to be topped up. In reality, it did not need to be filled, but I simply wanted a little more time to cool off before going home. The exchange of words from the charter was still with me.

While I was standing by the boat at the fuel dock, chatting to the young attendant, I heard someone call my name. I looked up and saw Cliff. He was a splash of colour in a Hawaiian shirt, yellow pants and white deck shoes. He was also wearing a porkpie hat and prescription sunglasses. I cannot tell you how pleased I was to see him. After we greeted each other, he said his usual stay with Alison was going to be cut short and he wanted to go out fishing before he left the following day. When I explained that the tides were all wrong and that I'd heard orcas were at Beechy Head and moving toward us, he said he didn't care—he simply wanted to be out on the water. Despite my joy at seeing him, I was reluctant to take him. I was certain we would not have a single strike and the trip would be for nothing. There was also the question of cost—he would have to shoulder the entire cost himself instead of having it spread over a group of people.

"None of that matters," he said.

I had run out of arguments, so off we went.

On the way out I contacted some of the local charter skippers by CB radio to find out how they were doing. The results were dismal—none of my reliable sources had seen a salmon in over two hours. With this information in hand and the orcas heading our way, I decided to fish directly in Race Passage off a rock we called RON Blasting. The rock was so named because a notice was written directly on it to warn boaters the peninsula was used by the Royal Canadian Navy to explode ordnance. The large letters were supposed to read RCN Blasting, but instead they appeared to read RON Blasting.

When we reached RON, I pulled out two medium-weight spinning rods with two saltwater spinning reels and attached forty-gram herring lures. I explained to Cliff that we would drift slowly past this rock, fishing at a depth of thirty pulls. A pull represents about two feet. With no other boats in the vicinity we had an unobstructed drift.

This is one of my favourite ways of fishing. The engine is turned off and each fisherman has his own rod and feels the moment a fish strikes. On this afternoon the sun was hot and the water inactive so our hundred-yard drifts lasted about twenty minutes before we pulled in our lines and returned to our starting point.

We talked of politics, grumbling about the poor quality of candidates. Religion floated into the conversation, and we both complained about the poor choice all gods had made when they moulded humans. We talked of family and nearly came to tears trying to express how much we loved our children. We talked of death and how final and pointless it seemed.

We were so deep in conversation I nearly choked on the dolmades I was eating when Cliff snapped his rod up and shouted, "Fish on!" His rod doubled over. "Maybe I've just got bottom."

"If you have bottom, the bottom is moving." I put down my rod to check the drag on Cliff's reel. As I did the salmon took its first run, racing to the surface and heading toward Victoria. We looked at each other. I shook my head, saying, "If this is another thirty pounder, you'll be on permanent staff."

"I think you just hired me."

Working a fifty-foot cruiser when you are alone can be a bit tricky. Sten and I were such a team we scarcely noticed how we covered for each other. But today I was on my own. I cranked in my line, started the engine and slipped us into a slow reverse.

"Watch out," I yelled to Cliff. "I've put her in reverse, so don't let your line go slack."

Cliff was ahead of me, bringing in line as fast as he could.

"I'll put us in neutral as soon as it stops running."

"Better do it now," he called up to me. "It's sounding and coming back."

I put the boat in neutral and pressed the kill button on the engine. In the silence all I could hear was Cliff mumbling under his breath as he reeled in the slack line. We were in deep water at the mouth of the bay with a light breeze pushing us toward Victoria. This was a fabulous spot to play the salmon.

"It's a heavy fish, bigger than the others." Cliff was short of breath as he spoke.

"How much bigger?"

"Much bigger." He was puffing hard and his legs looked like vibrating cello strings.

I unfolded the director's chair and eased Cliff backward into its seat.

"Thanks. That feels better," he said, but he was still puffing.

The boat drifted in the slack current and the sounds of the barking sea lions could be heard in the distance.

"It's so nice out here. Even better with a fish on."

"Listen, Cliff, if you want me to give you a break, let me know. This might be a long haul."

"Now, don't you start with that. It's not often everything is perfect." There was a silence before he said, "Listen to those damn seals—you'd think they could learn something new to say. It always sounds as though they're repeating the same thing."

We played the fish for over forty minutes. At one stage I held my index finger under the rod tip to take the strain off Cliff's arms and shoulders. He didn't object so I knew it was giving him a break. For the last few minutes of the battle, Cliff stood up to direct the salmon into the net. He was clearly relieved the struggle was over.

Together we weighed the fish. When I told him it was a fraction over thirty pounds, he said, "I must be getting old. I could have sworn it would go forty."

With the boat drifting gently, Cliff watched me as I cleaned his salmon and slid it into the fresh ice left over from the morning's charter. He knew about the group we had taken out in the morning.

"How would you like me to take this fish around to those arseholes and stick it up their noses?"

I pitched over, laughing. It was the right thing to say at just the right time. Somehow it lightened my life. I shook his hand and thanked him. He didn't release my hand but held it until I looked back into his eyes. "Thank you, my friend," I said, "for an unforgettable day."

"No. Thank *you*, Peter."

We stood there, looking deep into each other. I realized he was saying goodbye. I let go of his hand and put an arm around him and gave him a squeeze.

When I told him to sit down while I took us back to RON he suggested we call it a day. "Let's end it on a perfect note."

So I packed up the tackle, cranked up the engine and headed for the dock. I called ahead on the VHF so Alison would be ready to collect Cliff and drive him home.

Fortunately there was no wind when we came in to moor, so it was an easy job to bring the *Kalua* alongside and tie it down with only me working the lines. Alison was waiting for us at our slip and made a huge fuss of the salmon. She insisted on taking pictures of Cliff and me holding it up. She even asked me to snap a few frames of her and Cliff standing by the boat. I could see she was worried about him as she bundled him off to her car. As they crossed the rattling ramp to the shore, they both turned around and waved.

That was the last time I saw Cliff. Alison called me several months later to say the cancer, which had been diagnosed before our last trip, had taken his life. I knew Cliff would say it had been a good life.

chapter 3
Jane's Fish

A charter can bring together the most unlikely people, people who would otherwise never choose to spend four or five hours together. During these charters I try to find what I call "the locking pin"—some common element in their lives. The simplest subjects are children and jobs, but I like to find more obscure experiences. I once put together two men who had been in the same Japanese concentration camp during World War II; they had not seen each other since their convalescence and did not recognize each other when they first met on the charter. It was only after I had drawn a great deal of information out of each of them that the parallel in their lives became clear. Even when I pointed out the connection, they spent a subsequent half hour verifying each other's identities by recalling events that occurred in the horror of the Japanese camp. In the end, they wept uncontrollably on each other's shoulders without saying a word. While they wept, we, the onlookers, wept with them. The charter ended in a group hug with everyone thanking the two old warriors for their courage.

The first people to come aboard Jane's charter were Jane and her husband, Jeff, a couple in their early forties from Southern

California. This was the second fishing charter they had booked while on Vancouver Island. Their first trip was in Tofino, where they spent an exciting morning catching and releasing some magnificent salmon. It was so much fun they decided to splurge on a second charter. I said a quiet thank you to the skipper of the Tofino charter and reminded this couple that unlike the weather in Tofino, here it was clear and hot. Jane produced a jumbo tube of sunblock and assured me that as Southern Californians they knew what the sun could do.

"Good," I said. "Be sure to wash your hands with soap and water after applying the cream and keep your hats on." They were wearing identical khaki slacks with identical white shirts, and to the amusement of the other guests, they wore identical floppy hats with their names on them. Jane was tall, around five foot eleven, while Jeff was slightly over six feet. Probably in their early forties, they looked athletic and made a handsome couple who gave the impression of being content with each other by the way they held hands and whispered together. During the course of the charter, I learned they were both competitive riders and owned training stables outside of Los Angeles.

The next guests to come aboard were brothers. The first was slightly built, under average height, with a varnished, bald head, wild, bushy eyebrows and ears set too low in his head, which gave him the appearance of a melting Popsicle. He was wearing a blue and grey rugby jersey and a pair of blue jeans held up by an oversized belt that nearly wrapped twice around his waist. He introduced himself as Matt. His brother was short and stocky with a protruding stomach that did not seem to be part of his body. He wore brown polyester pants and a plaid cotton shirt so well washed the colours had faded to grey. He looked as though he had dressed in a hurry and might have forgotten to slip on his undergarments. Shaking my hand with a crushing grip, he introduced himself as Vic. Both men had well-serviced hands. *No fear of losing a rod overboard.* Perched on the back of their heads were soiled baseball caps that were obviously part of their daily wear.

During the course of the charter, I learned they were dairy farmers who had family in Alberta tending the farm while they gave themselves a brief vacation from the routine of work. This was to be the highlight of their vacation. *No pressure here*, I thought wryly.

Arriving last was a young couple in their late twenties. They looked scrubbed and starched. They both wore short-sleeved shirts with button-down collars, new white deck shoes and stylish shorts with so many pockets you could lose your hands in them. Their flashing smiles showed white teeth and good humour. They eagerly introduced themselves as Alice and Ethan. *Ah, computer nerds.*

I looked up at Sten, who was already at the helm monitoring the engine and adjusting the squelch on the CB. When he looked back at me I threw him a questioning look.

"I'll stay at the helm," he said.

"You're on," I replied in response to our usual unspoken bet.

While Sten cruised us to the ten-fathom mark in the bay, I gave the guests a class in Drift Fishing 101. I taught them how to strip out the line, how to work the reels and how to react when they had a strike. Once they seemed confident about how to use the gear, I checked them for sunblock and reminded them to wash their hands before I dispersed them around the boat with their rods. For about an hour and a half we fished around the kelp bed and the ten-fathom line in the bay. There was lots of bait in the water around us, but all we caught were dogfish and a few shakers, very young salmon that you can shake off your line. Matt and Vic were thunderstruck by the dogfish, which resemble sharks. Sometimes they're called cat sharks. They could not believe we shook them off the hook and sent them back into the ocean without ever touching them. I explained that a foot-and-a-half dogfish was more trouble than it was worth if you intended to prepare it for the table. The effort of skinning and filleting these small fellows produced very little edible flesh. In Britain dogfish are sold for fish and chips under the name of rock salmon, but they are the larger variety.

It can be tedious fishing under a hot sun when there is little activity. Many city people go out fishing with highlights from a television fishing show running through their minds. They expect to cast out their line and hook a huge fish that they will play expertly and land without misadventure. Fishing is a process, and you have to love that process. You have to be enthralled by your surroundings; you have to enjoy the unexpected appearance of wildlife and be excited simply by being outdoors. Catching a fish is your intention but the day should not be ruined if you go home "*bredouille*" (empty-handed), "skunked" or "with an empty creel."

After an hour and a half, with only dogfish and shakers to show for their efforts, this group was becoming impatient. It takes more than an hour and a half to make me feel like Santiago on his eighty-four-day quest. I called out for everyone to pull in their lines and head below deck for a cold drink and a bite to eat while Sten moved us to another spot.

Earlier, while they were fishing, I'd spent time talking to each couple, asking them about their lives. Most people like nothing more than to talk about themselves, and what I discovered was that everyone in the group shared an Irish ancestry. While sandwiches were being unpacked and cans of juice snapped open, I mentioned that everyone in the group had Irish ancestry. In no time they were comparing backgrounds.

While this was going on, I went up to the helm to have a chat with Sten as we cruised to a fresh location.

"I think you found the locking pin," he said.

"Sounds like it. It'll be fun to see how it plays out."

We relocated to a place on the other side of William Head. It was not a spot we usually frequented, but sometimes it produced a gorgeous fish. Once there, it was hard to get everyone out of the shade of the cabin and back on deck. The chatter among them was high-spirited. The brothers and Ethan had discovered that their distant relatives had both come from a town in Ireland called Sligo. Using my VHF, the Californians were calling relatives in California and Ohio to find out where their family had lived in "the old country."

The tone of the language in the group started to take on mystical dimensions. I could hear the words *weird, cosmic* and *strange* uttered in excited tones. Before they resumed fishing, the Californians had heard back from their relatives that Jeff's family originated in Sligo while Jane's family came from a town in County Mayo now called Newport. There was a boisterous mock reunion as everyone hugged and broke into jigs and called each other "cousin." At this point, Sten joined in with the rest, and loud cheers and a round of applause ensued after the group had clapped out the time to his dancing. I wagged my finger at him, threatening to incorporate his jig into all future charters.

"Performances cost extra," he said with a smile.

By this point, any remaining barriers among the group had come down. Everyone congregated on the stern deck. From the chatter you would have thought they'd known each other for decades instead of hours. For a while I thought they were going to forget the purpose of the charter, but soon Jane, clearly the most competitive of the group, was stripping out line and counting the pulls aloud. The sight of Jane peeling out line acted as a catalyst, and the entire group was soon fishing but this time exchanging anecdotes. The charter had taken on a life of its own, driven by the energy of the guests.

Within ten minutes we had our first fish on. Matt hollered, "I got one!" He struck so hard I was sure he had snapped the rod.

"It's not yours yet," I said as I checked the tension on his drag.

Out of courtesy everyone reeled in their lines to avoid tangles and formed a half circle around Matt. It was a stubborn fish, taking runs of ten or twenty feet before stopping and thrashing. Matt had his hands full allowing the fish its short burst before retrieving the line. Vic was standing next to me, shouting expletives at the fish every time it took a run. I had to ask him to keep the decibels down until the fish was in. Both brothers had told me they were experienced trout fishermen, which had led me to think they understood the principle of playing a fish. But Matt seemed so anxious to land it he had little interest in playing it. With a bit of coaching from me, Matt had the fish in the boat in twenty minutes. As soon as we dragged the net in, with the fish still wriggling in it, a round of applause broke out with shouts of "the luck of the Irish!" Matt and Vic could hardly contain themselves. They slapped each other on the back, twirled, slapped their own knees and shook everyone's hand. They grinned so widely I thought it must have hurt. It was a beautiful fourteen pounder stuffed full of krill, a tiny crustacean that looks like a shrimp.

"Goddamn, goddamn," they kept saying. "This sure beats milking!"

Having a fish in the boat allowed Sten and me to relax. In spite of the aesthetics of being out on the water, we could never allow ourselves to lose sight of the business aspect of charter fishing. A salmon in the boat takes the hex off the charter; everyone relaxes and fishes with more optimism. The most important thing is that the guests realize the ocean does indeed contain some fish and that they can be caught. Once a fish has been netted and landed, everyone's mood is upbeat. It's contagious. In this case everyone was shaking hands and congratulating one another as though they had each caught the fish themselves. It is a magical time of smiles and collaboration.

Pictures were taken of Matt holding the fish, of Matt and Vic holding the fish, then of the entire group standing around Matt with the fish. They even squeezed me into one of their pictures, but they could not persuade Sten to pose. One of his idiosyncrasies was that he did not like to have his picture taken. I used to tease him that it was because his picture was in every post office across Canada and someone might recognize him.

While Sten dressed the fish and put it on ice, I moved us back to our original spot and the whole crew stripped their lines down to thirteen fathoms. The chatter was intense. Alice and Ethan bet Jeff and Jane they would land the next salmon. The wager was for a dinner at a terrific restaurant in Sooke that I'd recommended. The two brothers chose not to join in the bet; they said they already had their fish and they did not like food in "fancy" restaurants.

Over the next hour, we picked up a couple of seven to eight pounders. Both were caught by Matt and Vic, who used their good fortune to poke some fun at the other two couples. Matt even offered to give Alice and Ethan a lesson in fishing and to change rods with Alice. She turned down his kind offer with a good-natured shake of the head.

Time to move, I thought.

I looked over at Sten, who was talking to Jeff. As soon as he saw my look he nodded, called for all lines to be brought in and went up to the helm, where he fired up the engine. This time we motored to one of our quiet spots. We used this location only when we were looking for a slug. It's a tricky place to fish and requires the engine to be left on to keep the boat in the right place and to prevent it from drifting onto the rocks. When you are properly positioned, you can reach out with your rod and touch the rocky shoreline. We used this difficult spot only when the tides collaborated.

Jane was the first to strip out twenty-five pulls. I watched her count each pull and set the drag before I turned to assist Alice.

"How many pulls did you say?" Jane asked again.

"Twenty-five," I said without looking back at her.

"You sure?"

I looked back at her. She was in a classic fisherman's pose. Her right and left hand were holding the rod straight up at ninety degrees. The rod was bowed, the tip nearly bent double, and her right foot was flat on the deck and her left on tiptoe. What made the pose classic was her straight back. For a fraction of a second, I took in the beauty of her stance. With the tension of action captured almost in a freeze frame, it had Greek proportions.

"Lines up," I called.

I heard the buzz of reels bringing in line, but I was focused on Jane. Her rod remained bowed; the reel was beginning to creak.

"Perfect!" I called to her. "Keep the pressure on but let him run." I moved as I talked. I checked the drag on her reel and lightened it slightly, which allowed the line to creak out faster. The fish was now directly at our stern and swimming away, about forty feet below the surface. Sten slipped the engine into reverse to move us away from the shoreline and the kelp. The fish was moving with authority, cruising away from the boat and pulling out line as it went.

Sometimes it takes a minute or two for a large salmon to react to being hooked. You'd think that a sharp hook in its mouth would attract its attention immediately. I could almost hear the theme music from *Jaws* playing in the background. With or without musical accompaniment, this beauty was going to streak out line as soon as it realized it was threatened.

I looked at Jane. She was composed but I could see the shivers going up and down her back and the slight trembling of her legs. She looked great. I knew that our chances of landing this fish were only fifty-fifty. The line was fifteen-pound test and the fish had to be forty pounds.

I glanced up at Sten. He held up four fingers. I nodded.

"This is going to take a while," I said to Jane, "so pace yourself. If you get tired there's no harm in asking for a break." She gave me a withering look that made me smile. "Okay, I want you to relax your shoulders and arms but keep pressure on the fish. Rest the rod butt on your hip if you like."

"I'm fine, Peter. How big do you think it is?"

"Forty."

This caused a collective gasp from everyone on deck.

Until then, Jeff had given Jane lots of space, but now he moved beside her. "This is what we came for, honey. I've got my money on you." He kissed her left temple. "I'll let the skipper do the talking. I'll be right behind you with the camera."

There was no time to answer. The fish had decided to shoot out of the bay; line was screaming out and spray was spinning into her face from the reel.

"How much line do we have?" she shouted above the commotion.

"Enough." Should it become necessary, I told her, we could chase the fish with her at the bow, but that was highly unlikely. I was sure it would stop, turn tail and race back at us.

A hundred feet from our stern it came straight out of the water, landing on its side. Briefly it thrashed on the surface. When Jane lost contact with it, a collective groan came from all aboard. I shouted at her to reel. She seemed to crank the handle forever before the rod tip dropped again and thumped up and down. She was back in contact with it. I tested the drag—it was fine.

"Keep your rod up and keep pressure on it."

"What the hell do you think I'm doing?"

"You're doing just fine. Keep it up."

The fish gave line and took line, but gradually its runs became shorter and it spent time cruising around the boat ten feet below the surface. Everyone knows water magnifies. When the salmon came close to the surface it looked like a young orca, and questions arose about whether the landing net was big enough or whether it was a shark. Sten and I kept our peace and let the group speculate. Jane had been on her feet playing this fish for nearly forty minutes and her right arm was starting to shake. Each time the fish took another run, she exhaled in exasperation.

When the salmon slipped past the stern of the boat, barely two feet under water, I saw that the lure was across its mouth and that the knot looked worn. I was sure the line would not take another run, so I signalled to Sten to wet the net and prepare to bring the fish on board.

A good man on the net is as important as the fisherman. Sten was a master. In all the years we fished together, I never saw him knock a fish off a line. To be skilled with the net means anticipating the movement of the fish so that the net is placed in front of it at the right moment. If this is done properly, the fish will swim headfirst into the net and to the bottom of the basket.

I explained to Jane how she should slowly lift the head of the fish so it was just under the surface, then steer it toward Sten. "He'll do the rest."

The netting was anticlimactic. Jane steered the fish smoothly toward Sten, who dipped the net in front of it and allowed it to swim into the mesh. In a single motion he locked the salmon in and swung it on board. It looked huge and gave off the characteristic sharp smell of a chinook.

While Sten tended to the fish, I took the rod from Jane's hand and gave her a hug. The boat erupted in another roar of applause.

Jeff grabbed Jane and gave her a serious kiss, which turned up the applause even more. We slapped each other on the back and shook hands. It was better than Hogmanay in Scotland. Jane was elated but clearly in serious need of a cool drink and a rest, so I told everyone to go below and have a drink while Sten and I cleared the deck and weighed the fish. Out came my trusty scales, and Sten weighed the fish. It was exactly forty-one and a quarter pounds. When I examined the knot attaching the lure to the line, I was able to break it with a slight tug. We had been lucky, and the salmon had been unlucky.

Most fishing stories end with the netting of the fish. This story has an addendum. We continued fishing for another hour in the hopes that Alice or Ethan would boat a fish. As things turned out, they had a double header—they each caught a seven-pound coho. It was a perfect ending to the charter.

Nice people, good weather and excellent fishing. You simply cannot improve on that combination. And Sten had once again lost his bet with me.

After the fish were cleaned and on ice, we stowed the gear and made our way leisurely back to the marina. I took the helm while Sten pulled out plastic bags to store the fish—this was standard procedure. We were out of heavy-duty extra-large bags, so the forty pounder had to be slipped into a standard black plastic bag.

At the dock everyone clambered off the boat in high spirits, swearing lifelong friendships had been forged. Sten lined up the plastic bags full of fish and handed them to each couple. Jane wanted to carry her fish but Jeff insisted on doing the honours. It was probably a wise decision, since Jane's back was giving her some grief after the workout of catching the fish.

With a wave of his hand and shouts of thanks to everyone, Jeff picked up Jane's plastic bag and swung it over his shoulder like Father Christmas with his sack of gifts. Sten and I watched, incredulous, as the bag hit his back, split open at the seam and the prize fish slipped into the ocean between the dock and the boat. It was over in an instant.

Have you ever seen shock and guilt written across someone's face? Pride and jubilation were replaced with adolescent embarrassment. Jeff was so stunned he couldn't utter a word. Desperately he looked into the water between the boat and the dock, pointing but still mute.

Finally he found his voice. "Get it!" he exploded. "You've got to get it back!"

In unusual circumstances people respond in unusual ways. To my surprise Jane doubled over with laughter. She laughed so hard I thought she was going to do herself some damage.

Jeff was stupefied. Between them they looked like characters from a *commedia dell'arte* play. She laughed hysterically as he skipped around her, saying, "It's all right, honey, I'll get it. I'll get it back!"

I thought someone had rung a gong in my ears. I could not believe the circus on the dock. Jane was still laughing as Jeff, Matt and Vic peered into the water. The entire scene required only a fellow in a top hat cracking a whip to make it into a Dali canvas.

Clearly something had to be done. I ruled out taking the plunge myself or asking Sten to shed his clothes to retrieve the fish. It crossed my mind that a scuba diver might be around, cleaning the hull of a boat. Scanning the marina with my binoculars, I spotted someone who looked to be wearing diving gear clumping along the wharf. Running until I was breathless, I caught up to a young lad still wearing his flippers, snorkel and mask. Quickly I explained what had happened and asked if he would retrieve the fish for five dollars.

Without hesitation, he introduced himself as Larry and said he would do it for nothing, but I insisted on the payment. Before

I knew what was happening, Larry had removed his flippers and was jogging with me to the boat. He slipped into the cold water at the bow and for ten minutes searched underwater, only occasionally coming up for a breath of air. I became concerned about this skinny youngster spending so long in the frigid water. I was about to call off the search when he popped to the surface, spat out his mouthpiece and said the fish was directly below him, ringed by crabs, but it was too awkward to bring up. Sten rigged up a hand line with a monster hook on it and gave it to the boy, and we all waited with bated breath.

Within a few minutes the salmon was on the dock and Larry was standing at the stern of the boat wearing an oversized terry cloth bathrobe I had wrapped around him. I put the five dollars in the robe's pocket as I draped it over his shivering shoulders. The kid's lips were nearly blue but he was smiling with a fury.

"Wait till I tell my dad about this!"

He was shivering so much that I put some milk on the stove to make him a mug of sweet cocoa. While I was in the galley waiting for the milk to heat, Sten was double bagging the fish and giving Jeff stern instructions on how he should carry it.

"You've caught this fish twice," Sten said with a slight edge to his voice. "The third time it will deserve to get away."

Jane was still laughing. "It's almost a shame we got the fish back," she said. "Otherwise it might have given me a lifetime of leverage on Jeff."

Everyone came aboard again, poked their heads into the galley and said an enthusiastic goodbye before leaving. A couple of days later our local paper, the *Times Colonist*, carried the story of Jane and her twice-caught fish.

When the cocoa was ready, I called the young diver to the galley and put two huge oatmeal cookies in one of his hands and the mug of sweet cocoa in the other. I motioned him to the dinette table and asked him to sit down while he hungrily consumed his cookies and cocoa.

Larry was a chatty lad, eager to tell me all about his diving experiences and his favourite subjects at school. I thought he was terrific and let him chat and impress me while I washed the dishes, rinsed the reels and put the galley in order. Vaguely I wondered where Sten was, but I imagined he was accompanying our guests to the marina office.

In the middle of my thoughts, I realized Larry had fallen silent. When I looked over at him, he was staring into his cocoa.

"You all right?" I asked.

"Uh-huh." His colour was coming back and he now gave off only an occasional shiver.

"What's up?"

He squirmed in his seat then looked up at me. "You know you said you'd give me five bucks to find the fish?"

"Yes, and you did, and I did. We owe you many thanks."

"It's not that. It's something else."

"Okay, tell me."

He reached into the pocket of the robe, pulled out the five dollars I had given him and dropped it on the table. With his other hand he reached into the other pocket and pulled out a handful of twenty-dollar bills and dropped them on the table.

"You see, they all gave me money. I'm not sure if I should keep it. I don't know what my dad would say."

I looked at the young man with admiration. There was a lump in my throat when I said, "I'm proud of you. I'll bet your dad will proud of you too and say you earned it. Just tell him what you did and what I said."

chapter 4
A Mixed Bag

Some charters are remembered as distinct events, like the woman who was nine months pregnant and laughing so hard she could barely hold her rod while playing a heavy fish. We were in choppy waters, the wind was blowing and rain was sheeting down, so her laughter mystified me. To keep her stable I had to hold her shoulders from behind while she stood on a pitching deck and played her salmon on bulky trolling gear. When the fish was finally in the boat, I asked her what she found so hysterical.

"My stomach is so huge I couldn't find a place to rest the butt of the rod" was her answer.

Other events are not so much fun. I once had to pin down a guest and hog-tie him because of his violent behaviour. He and another family member had spent most of the night drinking, and they'd brought their drunken belligerence to the charter. The whole group was a problem from the moment they stepped onto the boat—most of them had also been drinking before boarding. Their family quarrel soon accelerated into physical violence. That was when I stepped in, pinning the most serious offender to the ground and tying him up. A trick in itself, that manoeuvre required the help of Sten.

As many police officers will tell you, in the case of family violence the family often turns on the person who intercedes. No sooner was this fellow tied up than I found myself the object of verbal abuse. The women screeched threats and the men crowded me, insisting I untie their relative. When I told them I was calling an end to the charter and we were going back to the dock, a huge outburst of anger ensued. The language was extraordinary and quite complex considering their earthy background, and of course I was the focus of their outrage. Briefly I thought I might be mobbed, so I pushed my way through the group and stood at the bottom of the companionway, which led to the helm. Sten had already turned us around and was heading to the marina at planing speed. When I looked up at him, he handed me what we called the Cardinal. An enhanced version of the Priest, it was a thick, eighteen-inch piece of gumwood I had turned on the lathe and fashioned into a mega fish bonker. I never weighed it but it must have been over two pounds; it was at least twice the size of the Priest. We seldom used it, but in this case it was just the thing to have in my hand.

When we reached the dock I used only two lines to moor the boat. With a lot of stomping, cursing and threats to notify "the authorities," the group disembarked. As soon as they were all ashore, I slipped our lines and Sten took us out into the bay for a quiet evening of fishing. We returned to the dock later that evening with a couple of nice fish and having spent four hours full of laughter as we recounted to each other the events of what came to be called the Nasty Charter. It doesn't matter what business you are in—it's inevitable you'll encounter a few nasty customers along the way.

As a result of this experience, I developed a company policy concerning the behaviour of guests. I made it a policy that on any charter or sub-charter the skipper could terminate the trip if the guests became unmanageable. In reality, most of the time we simply gritted our teeth, smiled and handed them the bill. However, we did put these people on a list of unwelcome guests and circulate their names through the hospitality industry in Victoria.

Once or twice during the course of a season, I would find it necessary to take a guest aside and explain that their behaviour came dangerously close to scuttling the charter. Most of the time they would apologize and calm down; most of the time alcohol was the problem. When dealing with the general public, you simply have no idea who is going to step on board.

* * *

When I reflect on my charter days, I recall some exceptional experiences with brothers. One afternoon while I was preparing for a late-afternoon departure, I heard a knock on the side of the boat. I've often thought this an odd way to attract the attention of a vessel's occupants, but practically speaking, what else are visitors going to do? There is no doorbell to ring.

I poked my head out of the galley. Standing on the dock I saw a tall, tidy-looking fellow with a full, well-trimmed beard and a white shirt, white pants and matching white deck shoes. He looked self-assured; I noted even his fingernails were manicured.

"Hello," he said cordially. "Are you the skipper?" His voice matched his appearance. It was a rich baritone with the clarity of a singer and just a hint of a Welsh lilt.

I have a soft spot for the Welsh, so I found myself smiling when I answered him. "Yes. May I help you?"

He made no move to board the boat, which initially pleased me. I like the ritual request to come on board. I assumed he was going to tell me he had some friends who wanted to come along for free or ask a question about saltwater licences. I was wrong on both scores.

"We're booked with you at five o'clock. I'm early because I'd like to clear something with you before the others arrive." He paused. "Would it bother you or the other people if my brother didn't wear his legs?"

I must have looked mystified.

"It's hard for him to walk on the dock wearing his prostheses." Obviously I was not responding properly because he continued his explanation. "He lost his legs in a forestry accident."

Ah! The penny finally dropped. British Columbia has a substantial silviculture industry, and serious accidents are a regular occurrence.

"Hell yes," I finally answered. "Legs or no legs, he's welcome."

"What about the other people?"

"It's their pick. They can either go fishing or stay ashore."

Soon the other guests arrived. I gave a brief explanation before they boarded, and nothing else was said. It was a great fishing trip and we all had fun.

The following day I was driving through Victoria on my way to collect some fishing gear from my wholesaler. As I came to a full stop at a red light, a thick crowd of tourists ambled across the street in front of me.

One of them stopped and waved. I peered at him, thinking vaguely that I knew him. I waved back. There must have been hesitation in my response because this fellow kept standing in front of my car and waving. He eventually pointed to his legs. For the second time in twenty-four hours the penny dropped and I recognized him as the legless fisherman from the previous day. Now he was wearing his legs and stood at least five foot ten.

Another pair of brothers turned up for an evening charter, and this time one of them was in a wheelchair. The way the *Kalua* was designed, I could see no way of transferring Jessie, the fellow in the wheelchair, onto the deck of the boat. Unperturbed, his ambulatory brother, Bryan, picked up Jessie and carried him up the steps and over the railing while I collapsed the wheelchair and carried it on board. On the deck, I reopened the chair and Bryan carefully placed Jessie in it. I waited until the other guests arrived before securing Jessie and the wheelchair to the aft deck. They were carefree brothers who kept us entertained with stories of the places they had visited and the experiences they had shared.

It was profoundly moving to see and hear the affection these two men had for each other and the daring activities they had engaged in together. They told us the worst mistake they'd made was to try windsurfing. When his board tipped over, Jessie's flotation device had barely kept him above water. Bryan had to scramble to keep his brother's head above the waves, and only with the help of another group of surfers were they able to reach the beach and safety. Jessie told us he'd felt like a beached whale lying on the sandy shore. Bryan assured his brother that he was indeed a beached whale and that he was lucky he had not been carted away for his blubber. The two brothers roared with laughter at their own joke. It was a grand trip, a few nice fish were caught and good company was kept.

* * *

Sometimes only a snippet of a charter is the highlight. It can be the most innocuous event. We were once contacted by a group who made the booking from Saskatchewan. They were a meld of two families and they wanted to ensure they had the boat to themselves. From my notes I know they turned up on time and that we went out into a blustering ocean. I also know that we caught a good many fish but none of any great size. This suited all of us since they were not experienced fishermen and they wanted to give away whole fish to members of their family when they returned home.

On our way back to the slip after a charter, part of our routine was to clean and store all the tackle before we moored and to wash all the plates, mugs and cutlery. During the summer months, Sten or I did this twice a day; it was just part of the business. On this occasion I filled the sink with fresh water and detergent and prepared to wash the table articles.

Suddenly I felt a light push from my right side. Standing beside me was one of the wives.

"I'll do that," she said, almost shyly.

I didn't move but gave her a smile. "You're on vacation, so go and sit down and relax."

"I can't just sit down and watch you do the dishes."

"I do this at least twice a day—I'm used to it. Besides, I'm a single parent. I do this all the time at home."

"It doesn't seem right. I'd feel better if I did it."

"Go on, sit down. Go over there and take a picture."

With that she went over to the dinette table, took out her camera and flashed a picture of me doing the washing. Some people return from a charter with pictures of fish, but this woman returned with a picture of the skipper washing dishes. I like these funny little bits of life.

* * *

We had hundreds of simple jokes that we played on our guests when the fishing was slow and a diversion was needed. When we drift fished, we would spread the guests around the railings of the boat and give them rods with weighted lures. If a strong tide change was in progress, the lines could be swept under the boat and tangle with the line of the person directly behind. When this occurred we would get the fisherman on the lee side to retrieve his lure, which brought up the other person's line.

Sometimes we would untangle the two lines and attach a beverage mug to the lure of the unsuspecting fisherman behind us. Before dropping the lure with the mug, we would give it a strong tug. The fisherman, with the mug attached to his line, would strike with fury and holler, "Fish on!" Pointedly, neither Sten nor I would pay attention to him. When the mug was finally reeled in, the fisherman would be given a serious ribbing. It was a childish prank but it always brought a laugh. Other times we would attach socks or boots. On one memorable occasion, at her brother's instigation, we attached a brassiere to the line of a fisherwoman. (I'm not at liberty to disclose where the bra came from.) When she reeled it in, she didn't miss a beat. "Ah, there it is. I've been looking everywhere for that."

Another time, we were close to the shore sheltering from a strong current while we did some drift fishing. On board was a loudmouthed couple who felt compelled to top any story the other guests might tell. If someone said their child walked at nine months, this couple's child walked in the uterus. If someone had a Cadillac, they had a Rolls-Royce. They could barely wait for someone to end a story before they would jump in to top it. Of course, because they were Americans, no other country could hold a candle to the accomplishments of their country—everything was bigger, brighter and better where they came from. After a few hours of this they were grating on the other guests, who came from several other countries. I moved the braggarts to the bow of the boat, explaining that I was giving them the best place. I sent a reluctant Sten with them to make sure they didn't return to the stern.

The engine was off, and the silence of the ocean around us was interrupted only by our low conversation and the occasional squawking of a gull. The fishing was slow so I kept the conversation active, covering several subjects. The other guests were nice, unobtrusive people who relished being out on the water. At one point one of them pulled on my sleeve and pointed to the couple fishing at the bow. The husband was standing with his feet planted apart, leaning back on his heels and reeling with fury. Sten stood beside him with his right hand behind his back and his thumb pointing down. Almost reflexively, I laughed out loud.

"What's he got?" I was asked.

I just kept laughing—I couldn't help myself. Sten was peering over the forward rail and shaking his head in mock disbelief. He stepped back from the rail and motioned for the fisherman to keep his rod tip up. Then he glanced back at me. I don't know how he kept a straight face, but all he did was give me a wink. Everyone at the stern of the boat got the joke at the same time. There was a brief burst of laughter followed by cries of support.

"Keep it up—you've got the big one!"

"Don't let it break your line!"

"Can I play it for you?"

All these helpful remarks were directed at the fisherman, who did not realize he was struggling with the bottom of the ocean. Unbeknownst to him, we had drifted into more shallow waters and his lure had touched bottom. To his credit he played his "fish" until the line broke, and he graciously received the condolences of everyone on board. The mood was light after that, and to improve matters, we were in the right spot when the bite came on.

* * *

I've booked only four or five charters that were exclusively for women. Most of them were pleasant but not notable, with the exception of one. This charter was booked at least six weeks ahead of time with explicit instructions given concerning what was needed in the way of food and drink. There was to be no alcohol, but cases and cases of a wide variety of soft drinks were to be available. As a favour, the party also requested that we pick up baskets of sandwiches from a local delicatessen.

None of this was out of the ordinary, and we made sure we had everything on board when they arrived for their afternoon trip. It turned out they were in Victoria for a convention and wanted to spend one of their free afternoons on the water. The fishing would be a bonus since none of them had ever wet a line. It was a chance to show off our local scenery while cruising around the stone lighthouse on Race Rocks and freezing their blood with lurid stories of activities at the William Head prison. We told them about a man's body that had been found floating in the kelp bed with his hands tied and his throat cut.

After cruising for a few hours, I suggested we might do some fishing even though this trip had been booked strictly as a cruising charter. Ten of them were on board and not one of them had ever handled a rod.

This, I thought, *is going to be a challenge.*

I imagine that if you have never done any fishing and all you know are the sequences shown in films or on television, the reality might prove to be quite different. I started my lesson very simply. I explained how our reels worked, what kind of line we were using and the role the rod played. I had each woman hold a rod in her hand while I simulated a strike from a fish and demonstrated how to respond. They were a bright crew; besides, the procedure does not exactly require in-depth training.

Sten had positioned us in the centre of the bay and shut off the engine. I spread the guests around the boat and called out the depth at which they should fish. The tide was just starting to flood, and a line of krill mixed in with a line of loose kelp was starting to sag into the bay. The krill were so thick you could see them dimpling the surface; however, I was unsure how deep they went. As we drifted past a fourteen-fathom shelf, Sten said the krill started at one fathom and went down to three. I had everyone bring their lines up to forty feet.

Just like magic, we had our first scream from the bow of the boat. Sten went forward to coach the shrieking fisherwoman. Another scream came from the stern of the boat, then another and another and another. In the course of two minutes we had ten fish on and ten screaming women. Sten and I were kept running, giving words of encouragement and brief coaching.

It was mayhem. Glorious, fun mayhem. The screaming and shrieking added to the fun and excitement. At one point I netted one fish and without emptying the net, netted a second fish. They were all coho, within a pound of each other. It was one thing for a duffer to hook a seven- or eight-pound fish; it was another to land it on light tackle. We landed all ten from that first run. Hooks, lines and rods were strewn everywhere and flapping salmon covered the decks. It took Sten and me a good ten minutes to sort everything, reposition the boat and begin fishing again. As soon as we drifted into the tide line, we had on another ten coho. The guests were swapping rods to avoid tangles and screaming with laughter. We landed every fish we hooked, and within an hour everyone had caught their limit of four coho each. I have never been on a charter that produced that kind of result in such a short time. There were so many fish it was like being on a commercial trawler.

Later, I was told that the sound coming from our boat carried back to the sport fishermen at Race Passage. While the guests cracked open cans of pop and added their private stiffeners, Sten and I cleaned the forty coho. The mood was like Mardi Gras. It was so easy to have people aboard when the fishing was great.

A bit of a surprise came after we'd unloaded everyone at the marina. They all took pictures and carried off their heavy bags of salmon with friendly shouts of appreciation. It was only after the charter, when the boat was washed down and in order, that I asked Sten how much they had tipped him. As the skipper I never accepted tips—they always went to Sten.

He looked at me blankly. "I thought they might have left something with you."

"No, not a penny."

"Hmm. Well, I guess that's another life lesson. What goes around comes around." Sten invariably resorted to this expression when something unpleasant was done to him.

That night I found a message on the answering machine asking whether four people from that day's charter could book for the following afternoon. Although I knew we had space, I called them back to say we were booked solid. When I told Sten what I had done, he simply repeated his mantra, "What goes around comes around."

That charter remained the highest-producing trip I ever skippered.

* * *

Along with charters that produced a large number of fish were those that garnered nothing. In our business, there were two kinds of nothing. The first was when you dragged your lines through the ocean for four or five hours without a single strike. During those hours, lures, depth, rods and location were changed—but nothing worked. I dubbed this kind of nothing "hand-grenade conditions," implying that only a hand grenade would produce a fish. To the initiated this was part and parcel of fishing. To the tourist who decides to try fishing as an experience, it can appear to be a colossal waste of time and money.

Thus, I decided very early in my charter boat life that part of my job was to raise the fishermen's eyes from their rods to the world surrounding them. Most of the time it worked, and I could see the transition from a goal-oriented individual to someone suddenly aware of the extraordinary beauty around them. It might be accompanied by a deep sigh, the dropping of the shoulders or a quiet hum. At this point of transition I sometimes said, "Pretty, isn't it?" or "This is my office"—something to acknowledge their change. Of course, there were always those people who refused to see the fishing trip as anything but a waste of time and money. In truth, from their point of view, they were right. They had paid their money and received nothing in return except a ride in a boat.

The second kind of nothing was the frustrating experience of placing the guest in the right spot, with the right lure, at the right depth, only to have them lose the fish because of their ineptitude. If a guest lost the fish because it had wrapped itself around some kelp, chewed through the line or thrown the bait because it was lightly hooked, it could be chalked up to misfortune. But when the fisherman refused to listen to instructions and lost the fish as a result, I had to restrain myself from using the Cardinal on him. Embedded in the minds of too many neophyte fishermen was the image of someone strapped into a chair with a crane for a rod and line with enough tensile strength to lift an ocean liner. Finesse and skill were not part of this image; grunting brute strength coloured the entire picture. I cannot count the number of times I've stood beside a fisherman and told him to allow the fish to run instead of trying to horse it in. Most people picked up on the technique quickly, but there were always those who deserved a Cardinal lesson.

One early morning I made my way down to my boat. It was well before dawn, and I was earlier than usual because I needed to sort out some tack and replace old spools of line with fresh ones.

Following behind me was a young couple. It was too early for me to be interested in engaging them in conversation. They trailed me down the dock to my boat. When I turned around to confront them I could tell, even in the poor light, that they looked a mess. Their hair was dishevelled, their clothes were in shambles and even the laces on their deck shoes were not tied. My first thought was that they were transients who were going to forcefully demand money from me.

"Are you the skipper?" a young, masculine voice asked in the dark.

I took half a step back and shifted my weight so that I had room to manoeuvre. "Why do you ask?"

"We're booked with you this morning. Do we pay now?"

I was carrying a list of names for the morning charter, and with the help of my pocket flashlight, I found their names on the list. I invited them on board, suggesting they sit out of the way while I prepared the gear and the boat for the charter. With the lights on I could see they were very young and looked rough and out of sorts. Unexpectedly the young woman asked whether the boat had a shower and if so, could she use it? There is a first for everything, and I could think of no reason to turn her down. They both piled into the five-by-five-foot head with instructions on how to use the shower and why they should leave the window open. Within twenty minutes they had showered, brushed their teeth and emerged with big smiles, wet hair and billowing steam because they had not followed my instructions to open the bathroom window. I had coffee and tepid Danishes ready for them. They were like children in the way they accepted anything that was put in front of them.

The touching part of the story unravelled as the charter progressed. It turned out they were newlyweds and had to make the choice between sleeping in the comfort of a hotel room or sleeping in their car and going fishing. They could not afford to do both. The young wife had gladly opted for sleeping in the car so that her husband could fulfill a prairie boy's dream of fishing for a salmon in the Pacific Ocean. The best part of this story is that he caught an eleven-pound chinook on ten-pound test. On our way out, I had given him the choice between ten- or fifteen-pound test line. To my surprise he selected the lighter line, saying he had done some fly fishing and preferred the drama of light gear. When he did hook his salmon it took a good twenty minutes to land. Several times I was sure he had lost it, but on each occasion it was simply that the salmon had made a run back to the boat. It was a great experience made even better when he asked me to release his catch. To culminate this perfect charter, two retired couples from Calgary on board with the newlyweds chipped in to pay for their charter as a wedding present.

* * *

Another flash of memory was an elderly fellow called Steve who turned up with his three friends for a charter. He was one of those people who did not exude good health. He seemed old for his age and moved with a lack of fluidity. His white goatee and moustache, together with his ill-fitting clothing and thick glasses, made me hesitate to accept him as a guest. Before casting off I made a point of asking him if he had any serious health issues. With frankness, he said he had been dealing with a serious heart condition for a number of years and had survived three small heart attacks.

The more I looked at him the more uncertain I became about taking him away from shore and the proximity of medical services. I asked him if this was a risk he wished to take. He brushed off my concern and insisted we cast off. I decided to take him, in part because my capable brother Alan was paying us a visit from North Carolina and was on board. Alan was an orthodontist, so if any problems were to arise, he would at least be able to administer first aid.

With Sten at the helm we made our way into the bay and started drift fishing. The first fish we boated was a scrappy seven pounder that was beautifully played and landed by a member of Steve's group. Half an hour after landing his first fish the same fellow had a nice hit from a fifteen pounder, which he played with equal skill and landed in about twenty minutes.

I really wanted Alan to have a strike but it wasn't to be. The next person to holler was Steve. Out of the corner of my eye, I saw him strike. He had the fish on but his drag was so tight he was in peril of being pulled overboard or having the line snap. I loosened the drag, telling him, "That fish is over thirty pounds so you'd better relax and let it wear itself out."

Despite my advice, Steve was one of those people who simply could not get a grip on the idea of allowing the fish to run. Every time I checked his drag he had reset it to a tight position. While this puts more pressure on the fish, it also put enormous pressure on the fisherman and the gear. He played the fish with hands of lead for about fifteen minutes, after which time I could hear his breathing becoming laboured, and he slowly began to lose colour in his face.

"Are you all right?" I asked.

"I'm feeling a bit weak—probably angina pain."

Alan, who had been keeping an eye on Steve's condition, leaned forward to ask whether he had any medication to take. At this point Steve's legs started to buckle. Alan stood and supported him from behind. I took the rod from Steve's hand while

Alan lowered him to the deck and went through his pockets looking for his pills. While Alan found the nitroglycerine pills and administered them, I played the fish—somebody had to do the serious work.

Within ten minutes, Steve was back on his wobbly legs, asking to play his fish. When I suggested Alan should play the fish since he had taken care of him, Steve would have none of it. In the end his rod was returned to him, though I insisted he play the fish from a seated position.

Netting a large salmon can sometimes be difficult because they are courageous fish and often battle beyond their point of exhaustion. This was such a fish. Steve would play it alongside the boat but as soon as Sten lifted the landing net over the side, it would find the energy for another short run. I could see the lure and the knot holding it to the line. Both the line and the knot were in pristine condition. For another five or ten minutes Steve played his fish close to the boat, and eventually Sten was able to net it and swing it onto the deck at Steve's feet.

The following day our local paper ran the story of Steve landing his thirty-two pound salmon in spite of his heart condition. Not a word was devoted to Alan's excellent care of Steve. Fortunately, my brother is the modest type and he didn't need any accolades. In fact, he would have been embarrassed by them.

chapter 5
Overboard

Sometimes I get an electric taste in my mouth or I hear a kind of awareness bell ring in a distant part of myself. It is a strange phenomenon—a premonition that happens without warning and that must be heeded in spite of everything. This peculiar sense does not go as far as to foretell a catastrophe; rather, it is simply a notification, an alert. I never dismiss these feelings. I simply file them away and wait for more information.

We had a booking from a local family who had been out with us a number of times. They requested exclusive use of the boat and emphasized they were more interested in a quiet, scenic cruise than a fishing trip. They said they would provide their own picnic but asked if I would have a case of beer on ice and only to produce the beer if someone specifically asked for it.

During the phone booking was the first time with this group that I experienced the vague pulse of the alarm bell. It was just enough of a hint to prompt me to check my ship's log and reread the entries concerning the family's previous charters. The words beamed out at me. It had been an "exceptional charter," the people had been "terrific" and they would "always be welcome back." I wasn't at all sure of what to make of my sense of foreboding.

When the day rolled around for their charter, I went to the Dutch bakery in Victoria and purchased two dozen of their delicious fruit tarts. I also picked up a case of my favourite beer. I invariably select a beer I like in case it is left on board and I am forced to give it shelter in my refrigerator at home. The fruit tarts were *un cadeau* from us to them. In my log I had noted how much they'd enjoyed them on their previous charters. Along with Sten, Christine, who is my life partner, was on board to help with the conversation and to catch a fish should we decide to do any fishing. I loved having her on the boat because if anyone could bring us good luck fishing, it was Christine. I can't count the number of times she hooked a fish while no one else was having so much as a bump.

My quiet alarm struck a few notes again when the guests arrived. Sylvia and Tom were local people, and with them were a variety of friends and relatives. Jill and Arnold were another local couple who had their twenty-year-old nephew, Paul, and his girlfriend, Antoinette, with them.

Included in the group was Tom's mother, Helma. She was a short, stocky woman with hands that looked as though they belonged to a stevedore. She wore a loose-fitting shirt and pants, and a pair of thick, owl-like glasses with pink frames. Her hair was wrapped in a bun at the back of her head and pulled so tight it showed the exact shape of her round skull. She reminded me of a gingerbread figure. Somewhere in the depths of me I felt a light shake and heard a single note from a bell. It was so real that I looked up at Sten standing at the helm and the heavy brass ship's bell hanging a few feet from his head. He gave me a strange look and shrugged his shoulders. I recall hesitating and thinking I should cancel the charter. When I prepared to cast off I hesitated again, but I could not give myself a solid reason so I made the decision to go—but to stay alert.

The first four hours were pleasant but unremarkable. Following the coastline, we cruised up the coast to Beechy Head, then made a large three-mile outward loop into the channel and eventually back to William Head. We saw lots of bait balls—clouds of herring that attracted a wide variety of diving birds—and we even picked up an escort, a porpoise that played in our bow wave and kept our guests spellbound. It was a beautiful day, ideal for a casual cruise with a nice group of people. When we reached William Head, I asked whether anyone was interested in spending an hour or so drift fishing. The tide was reaching full flood and I guessed we might get a bite at high slack tide. The whole crew agreed that would be a good way to end the charter, so we set a course across the bay to Race Passage. We would be a little early, but that would give us a chance to set out the rods and explain our fishing techniques.

On the way to Race Passage, Tom approached me and suggested that while we were fishing it might be a good time to offer the beer. His timing was good, so once we were on our first drift through Race Passage, I went through the guests and asked if anyone would like a glass of beer. I had only two takers—the young nephew Paul and Tom's mother, Helma.

At that moment, the current in Race Passage was almost unmanageable because of the large whirlpools created by the changing of the tide. But I knew it was just a question of time before things settled down and we might have a chance at a fish. The trick is to be early in order to determine where the bait is going to school, then to wait out the dramatic tide conditions. In any event, everyone was enjoying the noise and the drama of the ocean. The power is breathtaking, even more so when you stop and consider that this is just a minute demonstration of the immense force the ocean exercises every moment of each day.

At the helm, Sten was ensuring we moved safely through Race Passage, Christine was on the aft deck talking to Tom and

Sylvia, and I was at the dinette table selecting some fresh lures and chatting idly with Helma and Paul. Paul was curious about the lures I had selected, while Helma was wondering what the fish thought of the bottom of our boat. I sometimes wondered what orcas thought of the *Kalua*. I told Helma how they would often slide past our keel and roll to one side for a better look. While they never bumped us, you could see they were having a good look. When orcas came close to our boat, we routinely turned off both our depth sounders. After reading about their acute hearing, it occurred to me that the high decibels from these devices might irritate or hurt them. Helma was impressed with this bit of knowledge so I opened one of the books on the dinette table and showed her a detailed image of an orca's hearing organ. While she was inspecting the diagram, I poured Paul another glass of beer.

That's your quota, I thought. I could already see the effects of the first beer.

With his glass in hand, Paul made his way up the companionway to sit at the helm beside Sten. I thought that was a good place for him since Sten would not stand for any nonsense.

Helma pored over the book, her bifocal glasses forcing her to tilt her head up slightly as she read. She asked me a few questions about the feeding habits of these great cetaceans. I was able to tell her that not long ago we had watched a pod of orcas feed on the sea lions that bask on the rocks around the lighthouse. We had actually witnessed a training session. The females and youngsters went around to the back of the rocks where the sea lions were sunning themselves. A male went around to the front. At an unknown signal, the bull charged the rocks, sending the terrified sea lions into the waters at the back. The two youngsters of the pod were sent in to catch them, but after two attacks they had not managed to snag a single one. On the third rush, the adult females attacked and slaughtered a number of the sleek mammals, which they tossed through the air to their young ones.

Helma was fascinated with this story and asked me a number of questions about their lives. "Can you catch one with your lures?" she asked me at one point.

I scrutinized her face to see if she was pulling my leg. "Orcas are too large for our landing net," I said lightheartedly.

"So get a larger net." Her voice was dead serious.

I let the topic drop and continued shaping and tying the lures. There was a long silence while I wondered about her remarks.

Then that bell rang again in my head. I was so preoccupied I didn't notice Helma leave until she was nearly halfway up the companionway to the aft deck.

Something in the way she was climbing the steps rang another alarm, but I could not for the life of me identify the cause. I looked around the galley hoping to find a clue. Nothing! I had another quick look, but nothing registered until I looked at the dinette table where my lures were spread out. Beside them were Helma's pink-framed glasses.

I was on the aft deck in two strides but I was too late. Helma had thrown herself overboard. She was floating in the vicious current four feet from the stern of the boat, kept afloat by a large bubble of air caught in the back of her shirt. Sten had already put us in neutral and Christine was calling frantically to Helma. I lay flat on the deck, reaching out my hand and telling her to take it. Instead she did a backstroke with both arms, which took her farther from the boat. I called out again, insisting she take my hand. I tried to keep my tone conversational but could see she was paying no attention. My next thought was to retrieve the boat hook we kept along the starboard walkway. When I got up to fetch it, Christine replaced me, lying on her stomach and talking calmly to Helma, asking her to take her outstretched hand. The currents were fierce but the boat was making a lee on her side; my concern was that the current might catch her and suck her under the boat. Just then Paul decided to be a hero and jumped overboard to rescue her.

Two people overboard, both who'd been drinking, at the change of tide in Race Passage. I could not think of anything worse.

I called out to Paul to give me his hand, telling him I would give him a rope. When he reached up to me I wound the spring line around his wrist, knotted it and tied him to the boat. My mind was racing. *One safe, one to go.*

As I reached for the boat hook, I looked over at Christine. She had used a mooring line like a skipping rope and flipped it over Helma's head. The line slipped under Helma's arms, which allowed Christine to slowly pull her in. Three steps and I was kneeling beside her. I grabbed Helma by the wrist. She thrashed and fought me fiercely, but at that point it would have taken a burly logger with a crowbar to break my hold. Christine was still hanging on to the rope around Helma. I remember thinking nothing would loosen her grip.

With great difficulty, we pulled the resisting woman out of the water and onto the boat. *Both safe*, I thought with relief. Once on deck and back on her feet, she seemed completely unperturbed, as though the incident had never happened. I was so relieved I could not find words to thank Christine. I was certain that if she had not been there, we would have been dealing with a catastrophe.

While Paul was still dangling from the spring line, the rest of the group was gathered around Helma. With little effort and with his assistance, we pulled Paul back into the boat. His clothes hung on him in heavy folds and he was freezing. His fingertips and lips were already starting to discolour, but he was in no danger. That was when the full reality of the recent events caught up to me.

"That's it. We're going in." I barked. I know I barked because even Sten jumped. At that point I would gladly have thrown both Paul and Helma back into the drink and left them there to keep each other company.

Without hesitation Tom approached and agreed it was time to call it a day. He was both grateful and apologetic. "I can't tell you how sorry I am," he said, extending his hand. For a moment he seemed inclined to say more, but then he turned to join the others.

I'm not sure what I would have said had I been in his position. I admired how understanding he was with Helma, but I could also see the fire in his eyes. It had been a very close call; we could very well have lost two lives.

While Sten stowed the gear and steered us back to the marina, I arranged for the women to strip Helma, dry her off and wrap her in a sleeping bag. Paul was directed to the head and told to strip and put on a new jumpsuit I had recently purchased on a visit to my brother in North Carolina.

On our way in I asked Sten to change places with me. I needed some separation from these guests and time to let the shivers work their way through and out of my body. Just as I throttled back and took us down from planing speed, Helma manoeuvred her way up the four steps to the helm. The red sleeping bag was draped over her shoulders like a cloak and dragging behind her. All she wore were her undergarments and her glasses with the pink frames. Her hair's knot was still impeccably in place. I can't recollect all of what she said. In hindsight, I think she apologized, but she also said quite distinctly that she'd had a nice swim and could not understand the fuss.

I decided not to respond. I kept telling myself that we'd been lucky, but I also knew that in life you cannot depend on luck. I needed time to go over the charter and pinpoint how to avoid that situation again.

A few weeks later I learned that during the charter Helma had been taking some serious medication to stabilize her emotional swings and she was out of hospital on a two-day pass. Tom was unsure whether she had neglected to take her medication or whether she had taken too much—or if the alcohol mixed with her medication had tipped her over the edge. However you looked at it, we had been amazingly fortunate.

Back at the dock everyone piled off. As nice as they were, I was pleased to see them leave. Paul came up to me and shook my hand. With his hair combed and wearing my jumpsuit he looked like any young lad after a charter.

"Don't forget to bring back the jumpsuit," I reminded him. "You can leave it at the marina office."

He looked down at himself. "It's a perfect fit, a bit long in the leg."

We both smiled. I never saw that much-coveted jumpsuit again.

* * *

On two other occasions I had someone overboard. Once, I overreached while trying to net a salmon and found myself in the water holding the landing net with a fish in it. I thrust the handle of the net at a guest and pulled myself back into the boat in an instant. In fact, the whole incident was over so quickly that Sten didn't realize it had occurred until he saw me standing on the deck, water gushing from my pockets as I laughed at the startled look of the fellow holding the landing net. It was a serious event but I played it down.

Another time, my son, Ian, and I cruised into the inlet for a late dinner and a bit of a chat. He was in his late twenties and playing international rugby for Canada. We let the boat float with the current while we enjoyed our dinner and watched the sun as it was sucked over the horizon. The water around us was a dark cassis with flecks of gold, light brushstrokes of sunset red and dimples of violet. The inlet was so still it was hard to realize we were drifting at two knots. I am a fortunate father. I have two wonderful children and the unmitigated joy of loving them unconditionally. Quiet evenings on the water with my son are cherished events I occasionally pull from my box of memories to rekindle my spirit. This was such an evening. We spoke of all manner of things—events, memories, hopes and wishes. It was the kind of talk that can be shared only between a father and a son. With it go worries—worries and questions. Had I been a good enough father to the son I loved?

When the moon was up, creating a bright, shimmering strip of light on the water, I suggested it was time to go in. Without warning, Ian stood and dived overboard, making only the slightest splash as his athletic, six-foot-four body slipped below the dark blanket of water. Terror gripped me. For the briefest time I could neither hear nor see him; I had no idea where he was. Then just as suddenly, his head surfaced twenty feet from the boat and I could hear him laugh. I've always loved to hear him laugh. He had been in swimming pools since he was four months old and was almost as comfortable in the water as he was on land. But at that moment I turned into a frightened daddy and told him to get back into the boat. He just laughed again and splashed around long enough to show me that he was making his own decisions. He was right, of course, so I relaxed and smiled. It's hard not to smile when a person you love is laughing with pure joy.

chapter 6

Carrots and Cancer

Some experiences are so profound they never leave you. One splendid August afternoon, I took aboard a group of men from Holland. There were six of them, all bartenders, on a four-week vacation in Canada. They had picked up my brochure at the Victoria International Airport and decided to book an afternoon of fishing. In their hometowns they did a lot of angling, so there was little need for instructions. I decided to take them all the way into Saanich Inlet to a spot we called Chesterfield Rock; it had produced well the previous day.

It is a spectacular cruise to Chesterfield. The inlet, which is almost 130 fathoms deep and fifteen miles long, has sheer cliffs along one side. On this particular day the sun was bright, not a trace of wind ruffled the water and because it was the middle of the week, only a few other boats were out. I cruised slowly, staying close to the shoreline to let the guests see the deer resting under the shade of the arbutus trees. As we cruised past Sawluctus Island, we saw a mature buck lying in the grass with a doe not far from him. A bald eagle I saw often was on its favourite perch about two hundred feet above the shoreline. I made a mental note of its presence. One of our spectacles was to catch a

small cod, hold it up for the eagle to see, then whistle. As soon
as the eagle left its perch, I would throw the cod onto the water
as close to the boat as I dared. The eagle would tuck in its wings
and power dive to the floating cod. At the last minute, it would
swing its legs forward, snatch up the cod, crack open its wings
and climb for the sky. It was a performance that moved every-
body who witnessed it. Just the sound of the eagle whistling past
the boat at water level could drop your jaw onto your toes. I have
a magnificent picture that freezes the moment the eagle draws
itself from the ocean with the cod in its talons.

We cruised all the way to Chesterfield, where I did a trial
drift. The tide was close to full flood but still running in. I suggested we try an alternate spot until the tide was just right. Once
the guests were outfitted with a rod and fishing at the right depth,
I went below to get a quick bite to eat and to fetch some coffee
for the group. As I was pouring the mugs of coffee, I took a bite
from a raw carrot. Inexplicably, I inhaled as I bit off a chunk. The
effect was instantaneous. One second I was happy and content,
having a great time doing what I enjoyed, and the next instant I
was unable to breathe, with a coffin lid lowering itself over my
face. In years gone by I was a competitive swimmer, so holding
my breath was not a foreign idea to me. As I started up the companionway, I thought, *No, I can clear this myself*. I didn't want to
upset the guests.

I tried every breath-holding trick in my repertoire. I could
not budge the obstruction. In desperation I went into the forward
cabin and dropped my diaphragm onto the back of a chair, but
nothing changed. I did this several times to no effect. All the
while, my mind was flashing with different scenarios. If I died,
would these fellows know how to start the boat and return to the
marina? Did they know how to use a VHF or CB? Questions piled
on questions as I slammed myself against the back of the chair.

For an instant I was able to take half a breath. It was enough to make me realize I had to involve the guests. As I made my way up the companionway I got another half breath, but I could tell my vision was starting to narrow. *Tunnel vision—not a good sign.*

On the deck, I stumbled over to one of the fishermen and turned him around to face me. I backed into his chest and put his arms around my waist and simulated the Heimlich manoeuvre. He didn't hesitate a second. He clasped his hands together, placed them below my xiphoid process and gave a series of upward jerks. By then I was nearly doubled over and half unconscious. Nothing changed; I was certain I was going to die. I clearly remember thinking this was a good place to die. It was a lovely day. I saw no distant lights, no chorus of angels, no cracking of a demonic tail. There was only quiet and a great sense of peace. I was on the verge of tipping over to the other side, of letting go of my present, when my lungs suddenly filled to capacity with clean, pure air and I was breathing again. The piece of carrot had been dislodged. In one instant I went from one reality to another. I was seated on the transom with six Dutchmen grinning down at me.

"Jeez, what a fella will do for a beer," one of them said. They were practically dancing around me as they laughed in relief. They had been far more frightened than I was.

I felt fine. I went through no recuperation period. One moment I was dying of asphyxiation, and the next I was wondering whether the coffee in the mugs was still hot enough to drink. I got up, thanked the beaming group around me and went below to fetch the still-warm coffee.

We had a good afternoon and evening of fishing. We caught some nice fish off Chesterfield, dawdled on the water and did not return to the marina until dark, when I had to use the searchlight to moor. During the course of our conversation I learned that each member of the group was certified in CPR; it was a requirement where they worked. I could not have picked a better group of men to help me that day.

It took me nearly a year to realize how those few minutes had changed me. I have never been one of those people who has a terror of death. Moreover, my death, whenever it might come, is not cushioned with the thought of an afterlife or of a spirit moving from a state of being to a state of non-being. What I experienced was very much like a dress rehearsal for death—the state of dying without actually dying. I had reached the point where death was within my grasp. But there was no mystery, no panic, no concern. Death itself is nothing to me—only the thought of the process of dying continues to give me some angst. I don't want a death forestalled by heroic medical procedures. I also think we should all be allowed to choose the time and place of our death, with or without a government-certified aide.

* * *

In this vein of thought, I recall preparing the boat for departure several months after the incident with the carrot. When the boat was ready, I opened the marina's security gate for some guests who had just arrived. As I greeted them and allowed them through to the dock, the last person said he wasn't part of today's group, but was there room on the charter the following afternoon? Something about him made me think he was special. Very often people who are born leaders have a special quality that transcends bland, book-learned assertiveness. This man had that quality, and I could not wait to have him aboard. I was a little surprised he asked for only a single booking—he struck me as being a father and a husband. I booked him on the spot for a charter the following day.

The next day he was again with the group of people waiting at the security gate. They had introduced themselves and were already making wagers on who would catch the first fish and who would catch the largest.

This is going to be fun, I thought.

We cast off and went straight to Willis Point, which I'd heard had been producing well. We were in luck because everyone aboard was an experienced angler and required no lessons. It was one of those charters where we had a fish on about every fifteen minutes. None of them were of any great size, just eight to ten pounds, but there was serious activity. It was a light bite, meaning the salmon were not charging the lures and taking a run as soon as they struck. It was more a light tap—the fisherman had to react almost before feeling the bump.

After we had a couple of fish in the boat, the atmosphere relaxed a little and the conversation started to flow. Life stories were exchanged, pictures of children pulled out of wallets and travel experiences told. Luke, the man I had booked the day before, joined in the general conversation in a quiet tone. I had been right about him. All the other guests deferred to him, and when he spoke no one interrupted. When he told of his life as an army officer in the US Special Forces, there was no posturing, no strutting to give himself importance. I thought of him as a sad soul. I could not shake the idea that he had something important to express. He was around forty years old, about five foot ten and had probably been handsome as a younger man. As I observed him on the boat he looked tired, the kind of exhaustion that comes from a great depth. The skin on his face looked artificial; it had a stretched quality that made me think of the mummies I had once seen in the Cairo museum as a young boy.

There's a health problem here, I conjectured, deciding to broach the subject with him just in case he was on medication.

When Luke put his rod down and went below to the head, I followed. When he reappeared I offered him a mug of coffee.

"No thanks," he said. "The caffeine doesn't seem to mix with my meds." He had such a steady quality that it was difficult to think he might be in some kind of distress.

"You all right?" I asked.

"I'm fine. Nothing to worry about."

"What are you on?"

"Morphine."

I was caught thinking in the wrong direction and could only come up with one explanation. "Cancer?" I blurted.

"Pancreatic."

"Shit!" The expletive escaped me.

"No, cancer," he said with a smile. He told me why he was not surprised he had cancer. He had spent a lot of time in Vietnam in active service. Several times Agent Orange had been sprayed on him, and on numerous occasions he had walked through areas that had previously been sprayed.

"Not just that," he added. "For over twenty years, I really abused my body."

Not an ounce of remorse or complaint was evident in Luke's tone. He described his story as if he were telling me about a walk to his friendly corner store. He also told me he was married and had two children. They would be at the dock, waiting for him when we moored.

"Then we'd better catch you a fish," I said.

"Damn right," he answered.

We went up the steps to the aft deck, where Luke picked up his rod and started to fish. A stagnant silence hovered over the fishing group; they had obviously overheard his story.

Luke immediately picked up on the changed atmosphere. He stuffed his hand into his pocket and pulled out a five-dollar bill. "I've got five bucks US that says I'll catch the next fish."

That broke the atmosphere, and everyone joined in and put five dollars into this side bet. The dynamics of the group had been changed by Luke's disclosure. From then on, every time someone hooked a fish, they encouraged Luke to play it.

"I'll catch my own damn fish," he would say, but he never did. Everyone else on the boat caught their limit, although most of them returned their fish to the sea. Luke had no strike in spite of changing lures and rods. I would have kept them out later, but he told me his wife and children were waiting for him and would start to worry. I returned to the dock with a sense of failure. Everyone on the boat was demure; there wasn't the usual boisterous atmosphere so common following a successful day of fishing. As I secured the boat I heard a woman's voice call out to us.

"Luke, did you catch one?"

"No." His answer was flat, noncommittal.

I hesitated. "Did you have fun, at least?"

"It was a great trip." I think he meant it—he seemed to enjoy the good luck of the other fisherman and was pleased they had done well. We shook hands. There was that silent moment when the turmoil of *The Iliad* and *The Odyssey* passed between us.

"Take care of yourselves," I said. "You're always welcome aboard."

He walked along the dock to join his wife and children, who were waiting for him on the other side of the security gate. Turning back, he said, "Thank you. I know you mean it."

The following day I was on the boat doing my usual chores when I heard someone call my name. I went up to the helm to see who it was. Standing at the security gate was Luke, his family with him.

"*Quelle surprise,*" I thought. I was pleased to see him. When I reached him, he asked whether I had room for one more. Little did he know that I would have gladly tossed someone else off the boat for the pleasure of taking him out again. He was early so I suggested he take a seat in the galley and have a juice while I put out the gear.

As he drank his juice, he filled me in on his life. He recounted the long story about meeting his wife and the birth of his two children. How he regretted not being present at their births and the problems his youngest had in the first few months of her life. He talked extensively about Vietnam and voiced his admiration of the Vietnamese, but he had no regrets about the military stance his country had taken in Vietnam. He was certain the domino theory was correct and that his actions were supporting the cause of freedom in the world.

I kept my thoughts to myself because our ideas were diametrically opposed. There was nothing to be achieved by airing my views, so instead I found common ground. I was born in Hanoi, Indochina, I said, just before the Japanese invasion. I told him how our family had returned to Saigon after World War II and that my brother and I attended a *lycée* there until it had been targeted by the Vietminh. I wondered whether Luke knew the area where we'd lived, and it turned out we had one landmark in common—Hotel Continental, which had housed our family for three months. What Luke and I shared was affection for the people of Vietnam and their culture.

By the time the other guests arrived, Luke and I were on firm footing. I told him that even if I had to roll a hand grenade overboard, he was going to catch a salmon.

"I would really like that," he replied, almost to himself.

Since the fishing had been so good off Willis Point the previous day and my reliable contacts on the CB assured me fish were still plentiful in the area, I decided to give it another try.

The day developed much like the previous one. We were landing a salmon almost every fifteen minutes and the bite was light—all our fish were between eight and ten pounds. Luke had several bumps but could not hook one.

I hadn't been fishing up until then, but I thought it was time for me to start. When Luke went to the head to administer his medication, I explained to everyone that he was ill with cancer and that if I hooked a fish I was going to pass my rod to him. A wave of sympathy passed among the men; the whole group agreed they would not expect me to pass my rod to any of them. But as circumstances would have it, I was kept busy netting and cleaning fish and I was not able to dip a line in the water. By mid-afternoon, although it was great fishing, Luke still did not have a fish in the boat and I could tell he was becoming fatigued—the process of fishing was starting to override the pleasure of fishing.

I knew when his wife was expecting him ashore but wondered if he had enough energy to fish that long. I asked him if he wanted to take a break.

"No," he said. "I'm all right."

I got up from my seat on the transom, walked over to him and took the rod out of his hand. "Take a break and have a glass of juice." Perhaps if Luke had been a healthy man he might not have heeded me. In this case he smiled and thanked me. I brought him a tall glass of cool apple juice. He spoke of the beauty of the inlet and asked what the factory was on the far shore. It had once been a cement plant, I said, but it was no longer operational. We both thought that was a good thing. Then I described a small river that gave into the inlet, a spawning ground for the salmon that was a struggle to keep clean.

Luke seemed to be keenly interested in all of it, so I brought out a chart that showed the shelf where we were fishing.

"Damn, this looks like a perfect spot," he said, sounding discouraged.

"Your turn will come," I told him. "Drink your juice and get back at it."

When he was ready to resume, I moved him to a different part of the boat, seating him on the transom. I sat down beside him and questioned him about the condition of Saigon the last time he was there. We talked about the beauty of the country and the deceptive gentleness of the people. As a soldier he was stunned at their tenacity and their ability to adapt to changing circumstances. I reminded him that a simple definition of intelligence was the ability to adapt.

He kept fishing while we were talking. I tried to keep him occupied and pointed out the various landmarks. It was evident he was nearly out of energy and would soon put down his rod and just observe the other fishermen.

Suddenly I could sense it—something was about to happen. Luke snapped his rod up, and it bent over and started to thump.

"Fish on!" he said.

A cheer went up around the boat and everyone, without exception, reeled in their lines. Luke had the drag properly set so the fish was able to run after its first effort to throw the hook.

Every fisherman I know loves the sound of their reel screaming out line. Luke's fish took a long run on the surface before turning around and charging back to the boat, forcing him to reel furiously to retrieve the slack line. Luke was grinning widely. I gave thumbs-up to the rest of the crew although my heart was in my mouth. I hoped fervently that Luke had the strength to play and land this fish. At one point it sounded, taking out seventy feet of line while Luke hung on to the rod.

"How much line do you have on this thing?" he asked.

"Enough," I answered.

Within five minutes Luke's body was starting to tremble, a glaze of cold sweat forming on his face. I put my finger under the middle of the rod to reduce some of the strain on him. Turning the reel's handle was increasingly difficult for him; it was going around in erratic jerks.

"Do you want some help?" I said.

"I might have caught this too late."

"Can I help you?" I asked again.

He didn't answer but continued to turn the handle on the reel. Looking over the side, I could see his line was going straight down.

"Let's pump this guy up," I said.

"How do you mean?"

I briefly explained how to bring the fish to the net using a pumping action. He caught on immediately. Together we worked the fish to the surface. At one point I had a good look at it. I could see it was starting to tire. Before I went for the net, I asked Luke to rest his rod tip on the railing but to keep reeling. I knew the fish was well hooked but Luke was too weary for any further efforts. The fish would have to be netted on the first pass.

Everyone on the boat was fixed on the drama Luke was playing out. None of the usual acerbic remarks were made at his expense, and no one offered to play the fish for him or to cut his line. We were all on his side, willing him the last bit of energy to bring the fish to the net.

Netting the salmon turned out to be a simple matter. When I looked over the side with the net in my hand, I could see it almost at my feet; it was simply a question of placing the net in front of it and allowing it to swim in.

Everyone cheered—I know I cheered. It was a beautiful nine-pound salmon. Luke was beyond exhaustion; he was shivering from the effort. I brought out a director's chair and eased him into it, giving him a cup filled with apple juice and covering his shoulders with a Hudson's Bay blanket. The chatter on the boat sounded like a parrot cage. Everyone crowded around Luke to congratulate him and shake his hand. He glowed through his exhaustion but I knew the effect of the adrenalin would wear off shortly. I suggested we return to the dock. When no one objected, I cleaned Luke's fish, removed the lure from his rod and handed it to him. He accepted it with pleasure and real gratitude.

"Give this to your kids," I said with emotion. "Tell them to come back in fifteen years and we'll use it to catch a salmon for them." I was nearly in tears so I went to the galley, where I washed my hands and composed myself. I fired up the engine and made for the marina.

In our discussions Luke and I had talked about Tet, the New Year's celebration in Vietnam, and how much fun it was. I promised him I would celebrate the new year with him in the coming year—the first day of the first month of the lunar calendar. He was stationed in Fort Bragg, North Carolina, and my brother lived in Charlotte, North Carolina. When I visited Alan at Christmas, it would be a pleasant drive down to Fort Bragg. Luke gave me his address with assurances that I would be welcome.

When we came in to moor, a woman's voice called out, asking Luke if he had caught a fish.

"Damn right," he said, "but it's so big we can't get it off the boat."

A cheer went up from his wife and children. When the boat was secured and the engine turned off, I walked with Luke to the security gate where his family was waiting. The rest of the guests trailed behind us. We parted with a handshake and exchanged quiet smiles.

"I'll see you for Tet," I said.

"See you then."

One thing led to another and my life continued to be busy. A month before Christmas I mailed all my Christmas cards with

North American addresses. One of the cards was to Luke and his family with a reminder that I would see them to celebrate Tet. Before I left for North Carolina, I received a letter from Luke's wife. In it she described how a few days after they returned to Fort Bragg, Luke's system collapsed and he died shortly after. She wrote that the last healthy thing he had done in his life was to catch a salmon on my boat. It had been a dream of his to visit Canada and fish for salmon.

Luke had ticked that box.

chapter 7
Some Fun and Games

Vignettes of my father fishing with us simply have to be in-cluded. My father had led an extraordinary life. One of his consistent pleasures was fishing, a pleasure he passed on to me. Prior to retirement, his job as a marketing executive with a large international oil company meant our family lived in many countries of the world, and he had fished in Kenya, South Africa, Vietnam, China, Britain and all through continental Europe. He was an avid dry fly fisherman, but he was also willing to sit on a riverbank with my brother and me, our bamboo pole and a float with a worm at the end. With a smile, he called worms "garden flies" just to give that form of fishing some distinction.

Dad was a terrific poker player. Two of his gifts were the ability to read people and the skill of disguising his emotions. These gifts helped him immensely in the heady business world where he had functioned successfully; in his family life he coupled this masking ability with his sense of humour. Sometimes it was difficult to tell when he was serious and when he was pulling your leg. On charters with us he had a terrific time exercising his love of hijinks. He took huge delight in rubbing shoulders with people who took themselves so seriously they thought the national anthem should be played every time they appeared. Men, women, children—no one was spared as grist for his humour.

Dad was out fishing with us one afternoon. Also on board was a crashing bore who willingly told anyone who would listen exactly how much he was worth and what an important person he was. All the other guests migrated away from him; Sten was dutifully and conveniently at the helm ignoring him, so I took the brunt of this man's bluster. Nothing could dissuade him from talking about himself and deprecating anyone who didn't have $30 million in the bank. I was pleased he had some cash and that he was a financial success, but I really wanted him to shut up. His self-aggrandizing verbiage was unending. I tried pointing out the osprey and diving birds; I even tried to get him to talk about his wife and children. The only subject of interest to him was himself and his vaults stuffed with money.

On cue my dad stepped in. Without saying a word he approached the stern, where Mr. Arrogant was fishing, carrying a quart of oil and a plastic spray bottle filled with a mix of detergent and water. We always kept the spray bottle on hand in case we spilled some diesel when taking on fuel. A couple of squirts from the spray bottle and the diesel dissipated.

Still quiet, Dad dripped two or three drops of oil on the glassy surface of the ocean. Immediately the oil caused a rainbow sheen on the water. Casually he screwed the lid back on the oil container, set it down on the railing and equally casually squirted some of the detergent over the oily patch. Instantly the rainbow sheen disappeared.

"I think this is the best batch so far," he said to me as he started down the companionway to the galley.

Our Mr. Arrogant nearly tackled Dad. "What the hell is that?" he said, grabbing my father by the arm.

"Oh, just something we've been working on for the past two years. I think we finally have the right formula." I gave him a hard look; there was not a hint of mirth in his voice let alone a twinkle in his eye. He was wearing his poker face. I looked up at Sten, who gave me a broad smile. This was going to be something to watch.

I was reminded of fishing with my father in southern England in mid-spring many years before. The chalk stream we were fishing had yielded a beautiful hatch of mayfly. I was fishing for a specific trout, which was feeding twenty feet in front of me, and I was having trouble presenting my fly in precise alignment with the fish. Dad watched me make a couple of casts before asking if he could have a try. I told him to go ahead. He stripped out some line and made an elegant drop just inches from where the trout was rising. There was a rustle under the water as the trout took his fly.

Looking at our Mr. Arrogant now, I thought, *that fellow has just taken the fly.* I had to watch this.

For nearly two hours Dad played this guest. He let him take a run then brought him in; just when he could have netted him, he let him take another run. It was masterful. Greed had clouded our guest's judgment. He tried all the oily tricks of a professional shyster. Invitations were extended as a snaky arm was draped over dad's shoulder, and he even began laughing at the most asinine things my father said. He practically followed Dad into the head. I later learned that Dad needed the privacy just to have a good laugh and to wash his hands.

When the oily approach did not work, bullying tactics were drafted into service. Dad was told that unless he cut a deal by the time we were moored, Mr. Arrogant would make sure this item never reached the marketplace. Dad suggested that perhaps a deal could be made and that he would be willing to give him a sample to take home without any written contract. Our fellow drooled. Dad said that, as an act of faith, he would allow our guest to run the sample through any laboratory of his choice. They shook on the deal.

"My word is my bond," Mr. Arrogant intoned as he pulled out his business card and handed it to my father. This expression wearies me—it seems like a cover-up remark for what people are truly thinking.

"We'll see about that," my father answered.

Nothing further was said of the deal until we reached the dock. When all the guests were ashore and the bills had been paid, Mr. Arrogant stood by the boat with his hand outstretched.

"You got that sample?"

With a smile, Dad produced a half-full bottle of Sunlight detergent, which he handed to our guest. "Tell your lab we use a twenty-eighty mix."

Sten and I burst into laughter. Mr. Arrogant was a dark thundercloud with mayhem on his mind. The last we saw of him, he was stalking back to the marina with his head tucked deeply into his shoulders.

For the next few weeks, Sten addressed my father as Mr. Sunlight. This became a code word we used when we had a difficult guest on board. One of us would say, "It's time to produce Mr. Sunlight." It is on these small experiences that friendships are built, and my father and I had a lifetime of such experiences.

* * *

With all the fish we have caught and all the experiences we have had catching them, size is seldom what we remember. Instead, we talk about the character of the fish or its courage. We speak of the long runs and how the fish sounded like a dropping anchor. We always speak of their beauty and the mixed feelings we share when they lie gasping on deck after losing the battle for their life.

There was one salmon we still call the Huge One. In fact, it was not huge; it became huge only because of circumstances.

My father liked to fish with us on wind-less evenings. Like most dedicated fishermen, he wanted to catch a fish, but the fish is merely the bonus that comes with the experience of being on the water under a changing sky and landscape.

The group we had with us seemed compatible enough. They were a mix of Canadian society—a corner-store owner, real estate agent, interior designer and two government employees. Seems you cannot have a group of people in Canada without incorporating a slice of government employees. It would be un-Canadian.

It was the first week of August, which usually produced some heavy salmon. The previous day had been spectacular, and even better had been the willingness of the guests to return their catch to the ocean. I hoped for the same results on this day.

My father came out on this particular charter in hopes of catching a fifteen- to twenty-pound salmon from which he would make gravlax. Our family preferred gravlax to the local smoked salmon. That size of fish is perfect for this delectable Nordic dish. The deal was that my mum and dad would keep one side of the salmon and I would take the second side to my home. Making gravlax was a week-long process; it had taken my father many trials before he developed his delectable recipe. We served it with a dill-mustard sauce.

There is a form of fishing on the West Coast called *mooching*. A strange word—I have no idea how it was selected. To fish in this manner you employ a long, flexible rod with a single-action reel. On this charter, my dad decided to initiate his new, special-order Hardy rod that had all the features of a West Coast mooching rod. Instead of fresh herring, he was going to use our standard, weighted lure. With such a flexible rod, it seemed unlikely he would be able to strike fast enough to set the hook. If he did hook a twenty pounder, it would certainly be interesting.

Just because the fishing is spectacular one day does not mean it will carry over into the next day. Such was the case on this charter. At first I was encouraging the fishermen based on the results of the previous day. After two hours of repeating the same drift without a strike, I changed our location slightly, simply for variation—both locations had produced superb fishing the previous day. I was sure the bite would come on shortly but could sense some anxiety in the group. As occurs so often, we had our first strike after a few of the guests began moaning that "there are no fish in these waters." After an exciting fifteen minutes, we netted a nice twelve pounder, and the "skunk" was off the boat. In the next hours we landed two more glistening salmon in the same weight range.

During this entire time Dad did not have a single touch. I started to rib him that his new, flashy rod had bad juju. Of course, he retorted that it was not his rod but the lures I had provided. We kept up this banter until he snapped up his rod and hooked a fish.

Before I could comment, he said, "Nothing special." Then he asked, "Who would like to play it?"

One of the guests stepped forward and took the rod. I could tell it was less than ten pounds, a good size to test the new gear. With lots of hoopla and excitement, the fish was played and landed by a delighted fisherman who said it was the most fun he'd had in a long time. His beaming face and shaking hands made us all laugh. Through this cacophony of good cheer I heard the whine of one of the guests.

"Yeah, I guess we're all glad he caught a fish, but I don't see why he got to play it and not me. I mean, I'm a paying customer too."

Ah, entitlement rearing its ugly head. A wet blanket covered our enthusiasm. I mentioned that Dad had made an open offer, and all the man had had to do was to step forward.

We continued to fish and to land some nice ones, but this character kept up his whine. A member of his own party told him to be quiet, which had no effect. Sten flashed me his signature eye roll a few times. At one point he whispered to me, "Do you think the Cardinal needs exercise?" I shared his sentiment.

Then, with exquisite timing, Dad whipped his rod up as he struck into a fish. The long, flexible rod nearly doubled over. He looked back at me and shook his head. This was not the fish he was looking for, but he had no intention of giving it to the Whiner—the man was just too irritating. Dad continued to play it.

Almost immediately the Whiner was standing beside him, peppering him with questions. He wanted to know how big it was, was it a coho or chinook, how much line was on the reel and the inevitable question—could he play it? Dad barely answered any questions. Clearly embarrassed by his behaviour, members of the Whiner's group insisted he be quiet. Still Dad said nothing. From his look of concentration, I could see he was getting a sense of the rod and how it responded.

"How is it?" I asked.

"Stiffer than you'd imagine when you strike." That was a good thing.

The Whiner interjected again. "I wouldn't mind testing that rod."

With this last remark Sten stood up and started down the companionway.

"I need you where you are, Sten," I called out to him. Sten liked and greatly admired my father, and I was sure he was heading below to fetch the Cardinal. He returned to his place at the helm but showed me his fist, a fist I knew he would like to use on the Whiner. I nodded but held up my fingers in a peace sign.

All through these antics, Dad had barely uttered a word. He continued to play the fish and test his new rod. From the stern of the boat I watched him work this scrappy salmon; he was playing it with a light drag, allowing it to take long runs then retrieving the line as it streaked back to the boat. The rod was behaving evenly from the tip to the cap, and I remember thinking this was a good addition to his collection of rods.

At one point the fish was alongside, about twenty feet down and thrashing, which caused the limber rod to bounce up and down. The Whiner thought this indicated we had a huge salmon in play. He edged so close to my father that I thought Dad was going to get an elbow to the larynx. Without any notice, line screamed out of the reel and the fish headed into the bay toward a black spar-shaped buoy. We were perplexed; we knew this fish was not capable of such a run. Dad held the rod straight up but it was bent at the ferrule at a nearly a ninety-degree angle. It looked more like a windsock pointing in the direction of the fish.

Just then, I saw the corner of my father's mouth turn up slightly. You had to know him to realize he was suppressing a smile. He turned to the Whiner and extended the rod for him to take. "Get a good grip and be prepared to hold on."

Without a word of thanks, the Whiner's greedy hands grabbed the fresh cork handle of the rod and nudged my father out of the way.

Line was still being stripped out of the reel. "Don't tighten up the drag" was my father's only advice before turning to me and winking. In French, he said, *"C'est un phoque."* A harbour seal.

Neither Sten nor I could hold back our smiles. Not infrequently a harbour seal will grab a hooked salmon and make a run with it, not realizing it is attached to a line. The harbour seal invariably wins. While this news was dawning on us, our animated fisherman was screaming for assistance. I thought I had better stand beside him to keep him out of the way of the other guests.

"Rod tip up and palm the reel lightly. If he turns around and makes a run back at us, reel like crazy." This was not a fair competition. I could tell by the way he handled the gear he had little experience.

Dad was on the aft deck holding a mug of steaming coffee. He now had a huge grin on his face. "You don't want to lose this one," he said to the man. "It's the fish of a lifetime. Maybe even a world record."

I could see the seal several hundred feet away, flipping the salmon in the air. Sometimes they play with their prey the way a cat plays with a mouse. It is frustrating to have been playing a large salmon for a half hour only to have a harbour seal decide to dine on it. In this case it was a small salmon with a twit at the other end. No harm was being done.

I stood beside the fisherman and murmured a few instructions while Sten assisted the other guests and kept them fishing. Meanwhile, the seal had taken Dad's fish into a kelp bed, where it was probably having a fine meal. No line was being taken out and only an occasional thump came from the other end to suggest activity there. My guess was that the line had been wrapped around some kelp and the seal had left with its meal.

The fisherman still had no clue about what was happening, and it seemed almost time to bring the charade to an end. I asked Sten to fetch the Polaroid and take a picture of our hero playing the Huge One. Once the picture was developed I suggested we cruise over to the kelp bed to see if we could net the fish, which I was positive had been taken elsewhere. I still wasn't sure how to finish this pantomime, but I thought something would come to me. Both Sten and my father had mirth smeared across their faces. They were as amused by my antics as they were by the Whiner.

Sten pushed the bow of the boat right into the kelp bed so the line ran straight up and down. It was clear to the three of us that both the fish and the seal were gone, off on some rock enjoying each other's company. The lure was obviously hooked into the kelp. After a few tugs we knew we could not release it. Cutting the line was the only solution, so I pulled my knife out of its sheath. The sight of the knife pushed a button in the Whiner's reptilian brain. Without any reason he jerked the rod up, evidently still under the illusion there was a salmon at the other end.

My father said, "Gently, gently," but this only spurred the fellow on to more vigorous efforts.

I did not dare go near him with a knife in my hand. "Lighten up, man," I said. "I'm going to cut the line so you can get back to fishing."

With a powerful upward pull, our whiner cracked the rod in half. It snapped above the ferrule with the report of a .22 at close range. The boat became still as everyone absorbed the damage.

I grabbed the rod out of his hand and pushed him away. What was left of the tip of the rod slipped down the line to where the lure was hooked in the bull kelp. I was left holding the butt and the reel and with an urge to use them as a bludgeon.

"How was I supposed to know the stupid rod would break?" were the first words out of the Whiner's mouth.

I was sure I would have to shield him from either Sten or my father. I was pleasantly surprised. Sten only shook his head and strung together some inaudible, private words, while my father simply said, "Cut the line and give me the butt with the reel," which is what I did.

Back at the dock, after all the guests had left, we shared a last cup of coffee. As we went over the events of the day, I was sure some rancour would be expressed. Instead both Sten and my father were philosophical. Sten said the Whiner should never have been allowed to handle the rod and my father agreed.

"My mistake," Dad said. "I knew he was a jerk, and the only way a jerk can behave is like a jerk." We finished our coffee and drove home with another lesson relearned—Gordon's Law: a jerk is a jerk is a jerk is a jerk.

* * *

At one point it became necessary to replace the engine in the boat. Once the new engine was in place, we were instructed to run it at medium revolutions for fifty hours to break it in. Halibut season was about to open, and neither I nor my father had ever caught one. I suggested that Dad, Sten and I cruise out to the halibut grounds and try our luck. In that way we would put some hours on the engine and learn something new. Aside from salmon gravlax, halibut was our favourite West Coast table fish.

Since none of us had the slightest idea of how to catch these magnificent flat fish, we inveigled one of the locals to come with us as our instructor. Jim, a retired commercial fisherman, said he would be pleased to join us. He would bring the appropriate gear and we would provide a fresh crab lunch. The deal was sealed and we set a date.

Jim was a living testament to the dangers of commercial fishing. Once, when he was unloading his catch, a load was dropped on him, crushing both his legs. He recovered well enough to walk, but he no longer felt competent on a pitching deck so he sold his boat, with its licence, and retired. The loss of his boat broke his heart, and now he occasionally drank too much and fell asleep in the cuddy cabin of his twenty-two-foot fibreglass boat. "Tupperware," he would scoff when talking about it.

As with most fishing, timing is critical. We were instructed that high and low slack tides were the optimal times to catch halibut and that they were typically found on top of a sandy hill.

We used our paper sounder to find four possible halibut sites and waited for the tide to change. Jim unfurled his halibut gear from his duffle bag and prepared it for use.

"Just remember," he said, "when you bring one of these big suckers alongside, don't lift its head out of the water. If you do, it'll sound. Just steer it to the stern of the boat and I'll put a gaff in it." With that he produced a huge shark hook wired to a section of a broom handle. About thirty feet of half-inch rope was attached through the eye of the hook. "I'll hook it with this then tie it off to a cleat, which will be strong enough to hold it. Next, I'll put another hook through its tail and we'll drag it till it's drowned. Either that or I'll shoot it," he said, nodding at his duffle bag.

I thought he was kidding. The idea of shooting a fish had not crossed my mind since I was twelve years old.

"I brought Jane with me." He pulled the butt of a rifle half-way out of his bag. "Don't worry—it's not loaded. Besides, it only takes shorts."

In truth, I did not know the laws in Canada concerning the use of rifles at sea. I hoped Jim did. A number of years ago when he fished commercially, the use of a rifle was not uncommon to calm a resisting halibut.

When conditions were right, we lowered our lines to the sandy bottom then brought them up about a foot.

"When you feel them take the bait, let them have time to swallow it, then strike."

This kind of fishing reminded me of fishing with a cork float. You can sit around for hours waiting for the fish to come to you. Of course, the monotony encourages conversation. On this day we talked politics and family. Jim was a staunch individualist who had no interest in government policies intruding into his life. His mantra was "Just leave me alone and I'll manage." He referred to the politicians as "a bunch of damn fools kissing the arses of damn fools." There was nothing subtle about Jim, which was one of the reasons I cherished his company. He never uttered a politically correct sentence and his words dropped out of his mouth as pure as silver ingots. His blatant honesty encouraged all of us to match him. Our conversation was open and blunt with no one taking offence.

Our political views varied from Sten and his left-of-centre position, to my father and I who picked policies from across the political spectrum. My father was probably right of centre while remaining a social liberal. I was more a centrist with a fiscal conservative leaning and a social liberal ethic. It was great talking freely without the company of saccharine types who oozed sweetness and light out of their lobotomized brains. At this point catching a fish was the furthest thing from our minds.

Sten struck up violently. His rod bowed but there was no life to it. "It's heavy," he said without attempting to reel in any line. The tip of the rod vibrated then thumped once. "Don't think it's a 'but—might be a ling."

Ling cod have been known to weigh over one hundred pounds. They look like giant bull fish with a formidable set of teeth designed to hold their prey. They produce thick, meaty fillets and are highly sought after by the local fishermen as table food. Usually bottom dwellers, they will emerge from their rocky habitat to feed.

Sten proved to be right. Within twenty minutes we had a forty-five pound ling cod in the cooler.

"I can't smell any more skunk," my father said.

"Let's catch a real fish," Jim added.

The conversation shifted to the beauty of the Olympic Range with its snow-clad peaks.

"Nice to see a snowpack this late in the year. It'll be doing those fellas in Washington State some good. Nothing better than a slow melt to fill the reservoirs."

We all agreed with Jim. Even the tall chimney stack at Port Angeles belching steam and smoke gave our panoramic view a breathtaking quality.

At this point the fun really started. My rod tip slowly dipped. I waited, it dipped again and this time I could feel the weight of the fish. "Feels like a 'but," I announced tentatively.

All activity on the boat stopped. As the line began moving away from the boat, I struck. Nothing changed—the line kept moving away from the boat and the reel spun.

"I think it's a good one." Since I had never caught a halibut, I was not sure what a big one felt like. This fish was moving with determined authority to deeper water. It was probably gliding down the other side of the sandy hill where it had been feeding. Like any duffer, I checked my reel to see how much line I had left. Of course, there was lots.

I walked over to Dad. "Take it."

"Don't be a twit."

"Take it." Line was running out of the reel. "It'll give me real pleasure." After all the help he had been to me over the course of my life, this was a small measure of payback.

He looked at me seriously. "You sure?"

"Go on, take it."

He smiled and took the rod out of my hands.

"Now, we're fishing!" shouted Jim. For some reason a round of applause broke out and we were all smiling. This was fishing at its best. Whenever I look back at this moment in my life, with the backdrop of the Olympic Range, Port Angeles with its tall stack leaking steam, the soft blue sky, the unruffled ocean and the black and white lighthouse on Race Rocks, it crosses my mind that those were the good old days.

Sten and Jim were concentrating on my father with undisguised pleasure. "Yes," I said, "these are the good old days."

The halibut proved to be stubborn, and I had to draft the director's chair into service so Dad could sit in it with one foot propped against the transom, which allowed him to pump the rod. Even with this configuration it was a serious struggle. After half an hour I offered to relieve him while he caught his breath and rested his muscles, but he would have none of it.

Grinning, he said, "Don't worry about me. This is what I came out to do."

But I did worry. Having a large halibut at the end of your line is like trying to reel in a living four-by-eight sheet of plywood with a mind of its own.

Slowly Dad worked the halibut to the surface. Our first glimpse of it came when it was two or three feet below the water. It looked so large I wondered how we would bring it on board.

Jim was pragmatic. "We're going to have to shoot the son of a bitch. It'll straighten the shark hook for sure." He went below to retrieve his rifle, returning to the deck with a handful of shorts in his left hand and the rifle in his right.

"Sten, gaff the sucker in the head after I shoot. It'll go all stiff, then you'll have a couple of seconds to slip the gaff into it before it starts to sink." He turned to me. "Peter, you get the second gaff to its head. It's gonna take the two of you to haul it out. Now, whatever you do, don't lift its head out of the water or it'll sound and we'll be here long after nightfall. Just steer it in my direction just under the water, and I'll do the rest."

To my father, he said, "Pop, you clear out of the way and let these two strong ones deliver the baby." With that he slipped a round into the breech of the old .22 and put on the safety. "Ready?"

Dad nodded.

"Okay, then bring her my way." Dad was so far from the railing that he could not accurately gauge the depth of the fish, so he guessed and swung his rod toward Jim.

There was a loud crack followed by a string of standard expletives from Jim. "Missed! Too deep—bring her up a bit. Better still, stand up so you can see, then bring her up so she's just under the surface." He ejected the spent round, inserted a second and slid the bolt closed. He left the safety off.

"Jim, careful!" my dad hollered. "Don't shoot the line!"

Jim roared with laughter. "I've got a loaded gun in my hand and your only worry is splitting the line."

Dad lifted the head of the fish and Jim shot it between the eyes. As he had predicted, it went stiff and shuddered. Sten slipped his gaff into its head and I gaffed it on the other side. Together we drew the vibrating halibut onto the deck, awed by its size. Jim pulled out his knife and dispatched it. Instantly all movement ceased. It was only at that moment we were sure it was ours.

We all congratulated Dad. The catch had put a real strain on him but he had managed it.

Jim was another matter. He looked at the lot of us then back at Dad, still full of mirth. "Fishermen are a crazy group. Here's me waving a loaded rifle around and your only worry was me shooting your line."

In relief, after all that effort, we laughed with him. He was right—we had to be crazy to let him handle a loaded rifle at such close range to us.

As always, the catch was divided between us according to our need. Jim took only a few steaks for himself. In the weeks that followed, Dad, Sten and I canned halibut, smoked some, froze some—and ate a lot fresh.

chapter 8
Rescues

Anyone who does any regular boating is bound to be involved in a rescue. I have both rescued and been rescued. Some rescues are as simple as giving someone a tow back to their moorage, a simple task if the weather is balmy. Unfortunately, at least 70 percent of the time on the ocean, one of the elements will work against you, be it the tide, the wind, the rain or the temperature. Sometimes all the elements pile up against you and place you in trying circumstances. The skipper of a charter boat can usually choose when he takes people out fishing. Commercial fishermen do not have that luxury. If the weather is stormy, with fifty-knot winds clipping off the tops of the waves, the commercial fisherman still has to go out and harvest the sea. The charter boat can hunker down at the dock and wait for better conditions. I tip my hat to those who use their skills to bring us fish and seafood that adds variety to our diet and helps to keep us healthy.

Slàinte!

Sometimes a rescue can be initiated by unforeseen circumstances coming together to cause you grief. However, many rescues are needed for accidents that are the result of blind stupidity. I am not even going to delve into the behaviour of rank idiots who cause serious problems by drinking while in charge of a vessel full of guests and family members. We should allow that lot to founder without a wreath over their graves. And very often the fools who disregard basic caution put the lives of their rescuers at risk. These fools should all be sequestered in a damp, dark dungeon until light dawns in their dim brains. This applies equally to the weekend boater and the commercial fisherman who loads his vessel with herring and tries to return to home port with only inches of freeboard. Toss them all in the dungeon!

Late one evening we were returning to the marina at full throttle. A storm was brewing and I wanted to be in the shelter of the bay before the wind started to kick up. We were ankle deep in twenty-pound salmon with two in the thirty-pound range. Everyone had caught a nice fish so the mood was light. I was at the helm and Sten was cleaning the fish as fast as he could. The group we had on board had been a delight, and to add to the pleasure of this trip, we had on board a writer, on assignment, who was going to feature us in his article. He'd caught a ten-pound chinook, a cause of ecstasy for him and great relief for us.

As we started through Race Passage, I brought us down from planing speed in order to navigate the churning waters and avoid any deadheads that might be lurking at periscope depth. Once I turned to port and into the bay, the wind slackened and the tidal action diminished. Race Passage is like a chute—tides are funnelled through a narrow channel over an uneven bottom at five to seven knots. The water can boil with activity, forming impressive whirlpools. Islands of debris can also be funnelled through the channel, causing problems for small craft.

Once around the point, I eased back on our speed to give Sten ample time to clean and bag our catch. Time also had to be set aside for pictures, so I decided to put us in neutral and pull out the binoculars to "glass" the bay and Race Rocks for anyone who might be in trouble. We often did this if we thought we were the last to go in at sunset. This particular evening I did not want to see any trouble. We were safely out of the strong winds and tide with only a fifteen-minute cruise to our slip. With the deteriorating weather, I wanted to be secured before the wind conditions affected the marina.

I looked carefully around the bay, then over to Race Passage. The wind was already starting to brush the whitecaps off the waves. My cautious soul was grateful we were safely in the shelter of the bay. As I reached up and clicked off the VHF, the CB was crackling with white noise. Through the static I thought I heard a word. My heart sank. I put the binoculars back to my eyes and swept them across the bay, then back to Race Passage.

I thought I saw a glimmer of metal close to the rocks, but I wasn't sure. The CB kept crackling above me before I clearly heard a faint "mayday" under the white noise. I fine-tuned my trusty Zeiss binoculars. I was now certain something metallic was glinting near the rocks in Race Passage. I must have said something out loud because when I looked up at Sten, he was already peering at me with a questioning look. I pointed at the rocks with my chin and put the binoculars back to my eyes. This time I could distinctly see a small metal boat broadside to us in Race Passage. The CB crackled again. I heard "Race Passage" followed by more crackling.

There were no other options. We had to go back.

I assembled everyone in the forward cabin and briefly described the situation. I explained that Sten and I had no choice but to go into nasty circumstances and that the guests could be off-loaded at the navy dock before we went back. From there I could arrange for someone to collect them and return them to the marina while we were performing the rescue.

While I briefed the guests, Sten executed our man-overboard drill, a routine we practised before the beginning of every season. Spare lines were brought out, knives were strategically placed, our boots replaced with gym shoes, life rings unsnapped and countless other small measures put into place.

Despite my offer, everyone on board agreed time was too precious to waste taking them to the navy dock and then returning to Race Passage, so they would stay with us to save the twenty minutes. We handed out life jackets and headed back to the Race, trailing our coordinates over the VHF. Their CB had gone silent.

Both Sten and I knew exactly what we were heading into. We knew the wind and tide, which we had escaped when we rounded the point into the bay, would greet us with full force. The tide was raging; we could hear it grinding as we neared the channel. We already had to shout to be heard.

Sten stood beside me at the wheel with the binoculars glued to his eyes. "Arseholes! No one should be in that water in a little tin boat like that. They must be from the prairies."

"What?"

"There are two of them. The boat is swamped."

"Do they have power?"

"One of them is trying to get the outboard started."

"What's the other one doing?"

"Floating on his back in the boat, not moving."

Without power, the twelve-foot aluminum boat was being sucked into the rocks amid crashing waves. We were close enough for me to see one fellow frantically yanking at the engine's starter cord. At one point I saw a puff of smoke as the engine kicked into life. The man eased his craft away from the rocks and toward the open straits. I was sure he'd seen us and would turn into the wind and tide and wait for our help. Instead he decided to cut the distance between us and run with both the tide and wind broadside to him. Waves slopped into the boat and filled it further. It was highly uncertain whether we would reach them before the boat was completely swamped.

"Sten, you take the helm. We'll load them from the stern. If their engine cuts out again we'll make a lee for them, take their line and ease them away from the rocks. Run both sounders. We're going to get them out alive. I don't think we can tow their boat so we might lose it. We'll concentrate on the people." I was talking out loud, more to myself than to Sten.

I cannot describe how confident I was in Sten's abilities. This was going to require some finesse under pressure. Together we had executed several rescues, but none like this. At such a time, fierce, concentrated activity was crucial. Under such circumstances, Sten was my man. It was one of the reasons I had hired him.

I went to the stern deck and watched as Sten positioned us, then drifted us stern first in front of the tiny boat. Its engine was barely making way, the pilot was cowed against the weather and his partner was floating on his back in the swamped boat.

I lay on my stomach and waited for us to be within touching distance. When we were just a few feet apart the pilot of their boat, a frightened man in his fifties, looked up. Grease was smeared on his face. His engine cut out. He didn't try to restart it but waded past his floating partner to the bow of his boat.

"Give me your bowline," I shouted.

"No," he said, gasping for breath. "You give me your line. Mine is short."

"Give it to me!" I shouted.

While Sten was skilful, he could not hold us stable forever. The fellow shook his head. We were still only a few feet apart, bouncing in the waves with the wind tearing away our words.

"Give me your goddamn line or we'll leave without you!" I yelled. I had half a mind to tell Sten to take us to safety without these two fools. Reluctantly, the man handed me a seven-foot bowline, which I immediately tied to the stern line Sten had set out in a large coil on our deck. I fastened it to our port stanchion and extended my hand to the pilot of the boat.

He shook his head again. "No, get my dad first."

"You first. We'll get your dad next."

He was exhausted and trembling from cold and fear. With difficulty I dragged him under the railing, then looked up at Sten. He had been a rock. With great skill he had worked us away from the shallow water and protruding rocks while trailing the swamped boat behind us and creating a partial lee for it. The *Kalua* was pitching furiously, buffeted by gusts of gale force winds. The swamped boat with the old man floating in it would probably founder if we tried to tow it. We had to extract him from his boat before heading for the shelter of the bay. Sten was needed at the helm, so I had no choice but to enlist one of the guests.

Several times in my life I have had to pick an unknown person to help me in a crisis. How my intuition works in that regard remains a mystery, but when I went below to the forward cabin, I knew exactly which of the guests I was going to press into service. I didn't even have to say anything; I simply looked at him and he stepped forward and followed me to the stern deck, where our first survivor was lying on the deck and retching.

Together we lay on our stomachs and pulled the metal boat tight to our stern, manoeuvring it so it was parallel to our transom. The old man was conscious and alert but still floating on his back. We poked and prodded him into activity, persuading him to kneel. When he was on his knees, we grabbed him by his belt and arms and hoisted him under the railing and onto our deck. He was a dead weight, his only contribution being a series of loud groans. Once we had the old fellow on board, we could start our slow journey across Race Passage and to the relative shelter of the bay.

I shouted at Sten, "I'm going to play out about thirty feet of line and see if we can tow their tub back to the marina. Slow ahead."

"You sure?"

I was as hesitant as Sten to drag this half-submerged dead weight behind us. If it started to sink it would present a serious problem.

I instructed our helpful guest to stand beside the stanchion with the tow line attached to it. I handed him my sharpest knife. "If I say 'cut,' cut the goddamn line as close as you can to the stanchion. As soon as it's cut, Sten will goose the engine to get away from the line, so be prepared." The fellow nodded his head; he was as solid as Sten.

With the wind and tide blasting us broadside, we crept across Race Passage and around the point. The tin boat stayed afloat but took on more water, which forced us to creep forward at less than four knots. In this fashion we eased our way back to the marina. On our way in, the father and son were stripped of their wet clothing and given some of my gear to wear. Before dressing, the old man was stretched out in the forward cabin and his blue limbs were rubbed to help his circulation. A grizzled old fellow with rough hands and rougher language, he showed not an ounce of appreciation for all the effort being expended to keep him well and alive. His son was from the same mould. Sten notified the rescue service that we were on our way in and in need of paramedics to check over the survivors.

At the dock a line of helpful men made mooring a simple task. They assisted in transporting the two survivors off the boat and to the waiting paramedics. As our guests disembarked with their load of bagged salmon and pictures of their adventure, I was of two minds whether I should charge them for the charter.

I decided to leave it up to them. I was not completely surprised when they all insisted on paying. The fellow who had been of such help with the rescue asked if he could purchase the knife I'd given him to cut the tow line. I was pleased to sell it to him—for a dime. I did not wish to cut our friendship.

The writer thanked us for his trip, saying he would send a copy of his article as soon as it was published. Most of the time I never hear another word from people like this, but this man was an exception. Over a year later I received a copy of his story with a reasonably accurate account of the rescue. It annoyed me that he did not mention Sten's extraordinary skill; instead, he made it sound as though I had handled the entire incident by myself while chewing pink bubble gum and whistling the theme music from *Swan Lake*.

We all shook hands and wished each other well. At this point I wanted everyone off the boat—I needed time to breathe. When they'd all disembarked, I told Sten to go home and that I would clean up the boat and prepare it for the following day. He gave me a long look, nodded his head and followed our guests along the dock to the parking lot.

I went below and began organizing the boat. Dishes and mugs needed to be washed, rods stowed away and the deck washed down. Halfway through these chores I realized the engine and both sounders were still running, so I went up to the wheelhouse to click them off. The paper sounder had recorded how close to the rocks we'd come. At one point we had only half a fathom under our keel. I sat there quietly, looking at the kill button to the engine. I couldn't seem to raise my arm to push down on it. I was too upset to coordinate my body and my thoughts.

This is stupid, I thought and reached out to press my thumb on the grey rubber button. I missed it on the first and second try before realizing my hands were shaking uncontrollably. My jaw started to rattle as though I was severely cold and my body to shiver. I tried pushing the button again but missed. My eyes were blurred with tears and I was sobbing loudly. All this was happening as if it were separate from me, as if I were watching myself from the outside. I realized I had been living on adrenalin for over an hour. However rational I thought I was, my body was reacting to the fear and stress. I tried to push the button again but could barely see it.

From nowhere, an arm wrapped itself around my shoulder and squeezed me, and a hand reached across the controls and pushed the kill button. The only thing I could hear was my sobs. I looked up to see that the fellow with his arm around me was the RCMP officer who had come down to the dock with the paramedics. He didn't say a word, just kept his arm around me until I slowed down. When I could finally take a breath—a deep, jagged one—I thanked him. I apologized. It was as though I'd had an out-of-body experience.

"You okay?"

"I'm fine now, thanks."

"It's just the adrenalin—it happens all the time."

"I know. It just caught me off guard."

"Can you lie down for half an hour?"

"I have to clean up my stuff."

"Lie down for half an hour. You can clean up later on."

"You're right—I'll lie down."

I stumbled below to the forward bunks and pulled a loose sleeping bag over me, falling asleep without removing my clothes. I didn't wake up until the following morning, and instead of feeling fresh and alert I felt as though I had been pulled through a keyhole backward. I showered, put on fresh clothes and prepared some breakfast. As I was having a second mug of coffee, Sten came aboard with a box of my favourite Danishes. Together we had coffee and the pastries and talked over the previous day. We had both been jarred by the experience and we had both reflected, separately, on how strange it was that life hummed along relentlessly in spite of the bumps in one's road. Sten could not believe how normal things were on his drive home. His experience had been so intense that he half expected everyone to know what he had just gone through. We both realized what a serious event in our lives this had been and yet, besides our guests and the two men we'd rescued, we were the only witnesses to it. In future years, it was a bond between us that we never needed to discuss.

* * *

The other side of the coin is when you are the one in need of rescue. I once needed a light rescue because we had taken on a bad batch of fuel that fouled the filters to the engine. The weather had been ideal and the tow lasted just ten minutes. It was slightly embarrassing but nothing of any consequence.

My nasty rescue took place one morning when Sten had a day off. I took a booking knowing full well I would have to do double duty with Sten ashore. The family that came on board was a charming group from San Francisco. They owned a restaurant where he was the chef and she ran the front of the house. They had three daughters between seven and nine years of age. The husband was a short, tubby Frenchman from Lyon with the soft hands of a chef and the sheen of someone who lives well. His wife was a tall, lithe woman from Ostend, Belgium, who radiated charm and humour and made it difficult not to smile when in her company. I liked them both instantly.

When they came aboard, they carried with them two huge wicker hampers of picnic food with the necks of wine bottles peering from under the chequered napkins. They also brought with them an easy civility that I missed in North American culture. Their children were joyful, energetic and openly curious without trespassing into the Brat Zone. I could not wait to have them out on the water to listen to their stories. Happy couples are easily evident; they live in an invisible hoop that allows others to visit but keeps them ever connected. This family danced in their own circle. They were a joy to have on board.

There was a hitch to this charter. At certain times of the year fog can be a problem in the bay. Usually it burns off by noon and leaves the rest of the day in bright sunshine. I'm always hesitant and somewhat uneasy being on the water in dense fog. We had no radar, so we counted on the good sense of the boaters around us and the use of foghorns to broadcast our location. On this morning the fog enveloped half the bay in a dense white cloud that extended through Race Passage.

While my guests made themselves at home, I cast off and eased us through the channel and into the bay. The fog was thick, so I decided to take a compass bearing, which would take us past the large buoy we called the Navy Can on our port side and straight out into Race Passage. Then it was simply a case of watching the paper sounder and following the shoreline, anticipating the shallow parts. I went past Christopher Point and into Whirl Bay, where the chatter on the CB suggested the fog was less dense but still blotted out the sun. From the helm I could not see the bow railings.

Not so good, I thought. We were perilously close to a sheer cliff and the ebbing tide was sucking us along. I decided to take us out of the bay and into more open waters, closer to the lighthouse, which was bellowing its position with an insistent voice. I made a hard turn away from the cliff and set a course for open sea. At that point, my only concern was other boaters who might not be advertising their position.

As I accelerated, the boat shuddered and grumbled through its timbers. My gauges showed no change. I wondered whether the prop might have picked up a sheet of plastic or some wooden debris. I put us in neutral, waited, then slipped into a very slow reverse. If we had picked up something, perhaps reversing gears would throw it out. But nothing happened—we did not even move astern. I put us back in neutral and raced to the removable companionway that covered the V-drive. The V-drive was torn from its bolted position and the shaft was sheared. We had lost all power.

My first concern was our proximity to the cliff. I raced back to the helm to check the sounder and check our position. I could see nothing, only the vague outline of our bow rails. I punched in the emergency channel on the VHF and sent out a distress signal with our position. The cliffs were still not in sight, but I knew we were drifting toward Church Rock. I thought of dropping the anchor to stabilize our position but decided to try the CB first.

Switching to the open channel, I sent out a mayday with our location. My heart thumped in my ears for a few seconds as I waited, then sent the distress signal again.

A voice boomed back at me. "Where did you say you are?"

"Whirl Bay, by the cliff. What's your location?"

The voice from the CB boomed at me and seemed to leave an echo bouncing off the nearby cliff. "We are alongside you."

I could not believe my eyes. We were parallel, bow to stern, five feet apart. A three-foot-long red sign that read RESCUE was attached just below his wheelhouse. To make matters even more inexplicable, it was an identical sister ship to mine without the added stainless steel railings. We looked at each other. I could see the CB speaker in his hand. The CB boomed at me: "Do you need a tow?"

I was so relieved to see him I could have hugged him. It was hard to believe how quickly our serious situation had been resolved. Luck is fickle. I'd been unlucky to have my boat's shaft damaged but incredibly lucky to be rescued so promptly.

"I'll pass you a line and feed out sixty feet," I told him. I rushed to the bow with a heavy roll of one-inch towing line over my shoulder. When he was in position I threw him the line and measured out sixty feet before tying it off. Slowly he took the strain, heading us out of Whirl Bay and back to our mooring with me at the helm.

Just then my French guest poked his head into the cockpit. *"Mais qu'est-ce qui se passe?"* Quite rightly he wanted to know what was going on.

I explained, very briefly, what had happened and our present situation. He took it all in with equanimity, gave a Gallic shrug and asked if I was hungry. I invited them all to join me at the helm, and together we devoured their picnic lunch while we were towed to safe harbour.

As we ate, their story unfolded. They told me they'd met at a convention of restaurateurs in Houston on a busman's holiday from their respective countries. Since they both spoke French and their English was laboured, they spent most of the four days of the convention in each other's company. At the end of the convention they rented a car and drove to San Francisco, where they'd heard from a conventioneer that a rundown restaurant was for sale in a stunning location. It was love at first sight once they arrived in San Francisco. While it was a far cry from Lyon or the famous beach of Ostend, they instantly felt at home.

Together they fell in love with the city and with each other. Within twenty-four hours, they'd made three monumental decisions. The first was that they would marry, the second that they would purchase the restaurant and the third that they would have two children.

Untangling themselves from their businesses in France and Belgium and arranging for the appropriate documents to enter the United States proved to be more difficult than they had imagined. At last, with all those difficulties behind them, they returned to San Francisco where they threw themselves into their restaurant and began building a clientele based on the excellence of their food and service. They quickly realized that serving *l'anguille au vert* was too ambitious. They adapted their cuisine to the local palate, gradually adding more demanding food with the finesse of French cooking and the portions of Belgium dishes. It took two years before they knew with certainty that their restaurant would support them. Their first daughter was born a year later and their twin daughters two years after that. Their lives had unfolded just as they'd planned—with a bonus extra child—but not without obstacles to surmount.

When we reached the dock, manoeuvring in required a deft touch by our rescuer's boat. He had to slide past our slip and drop the tow line, allowing us to glide into our moorage— all while avoiding the boat moored directly in front of us. Once we were safely tied down, everyone peered at the wrenched V-drive and shaft. We decided that a chunk of log had probably wedged itself between the propeller and boat and sheared the shaft either when we were in forward or when I put us in reverse. To me it meant a $3,000 bill, lost time chartering and putting up with the usual sour remarks from the marina about their lost revenue. Some things never change. I was just grateful we were safe and unharmed.

And there are silver linings to most boat mishaps. Each day while repairs were being made, the restaurateurs and their daughters came out to the marina bearing a hamper of food.

They spent the lunch hour on the boat before heading off to wend their way through Butchart Gardens or stroll through one of the many local parks. If you have lived in France and Belgium and travelled through Western Europe, young buildings like the 1908-built Empress Hotel in Victoria are hardly awe-inspiring, but the spaciousness of Canada is riveting.

They asked me where I ate. *"Chez moi,"* I answered. At that time, Victoria had few restaurants that produced anything more than US franchise food or mom-and-pop burgers. The exception was dim sum in Chinatown on Fisgard Street. Our family often had lunch there on Saturday and were never disappointed with their food. The trick was to arrive at the restaurant before they opened their doors at eleven o'clock and secure a table close to the kitchen. I passed this information on to my new friends. The following day they returned with glowing reports about the freshness of the flavours and the cheerful service from the staff who pushed the trolleys around the room.

Four days after our rescue, the boat was once again under power. The first group we took out were the restaurateurs. They turned up with enough food to feed the entire marina but with only enough wine for their own use since they knew it was pointless to ask me to drink while out at sea. While that may sound a little self-righteous, it was one of my immutable rules. I once fired a skipper for having a single glass of beer while on a charter, so I could not very well flout my own rules.

Sten was on board for this inauguration charter. He had met the family while the boat was being mended and decided he would gladly adopt them as his second family—a generous compliment from the reserved Sten. He brought each one of the girls a dream catcher and a one-pound box of locally made chocolates to share. I had seldom seen him attach himself to a group of people so quickly—usually he had to meet people several times before he gave his friendship. It was a touching thing to observe and gave me insight into the capable, loving father he would be one day.

We took them out in clear weather with the stack in Port Angeles visible from twenty-two miles away and the Olympic Range in full bloom. It was such a dramatic difference from our initial outing that they suggested the first time I had taken them out it was to a satanic lair known only to writers of hyperbolic fiction. We spent nearly the whole day on the water. We trolled, drift fished and simply sat around drifting in the current and talking about education, cultural differences and what we hoped for our children. It was an enormously satisfactory day spent in the company of enjoyable people with few emotional filters. That was the best charter of the season for Sten and me. We hated to call an end to it.

At the dock it was a sorrowful parting. They insisted on leaving the remnants of the lobster and crab from their hampers and gave us their card with sharp instructions that if we were ever in San Francisco we had to visit them.

With a wistful look in his eyes, Sten watched them leave. He stood and pondered for a moment, then said, "I hope my kids are as wonderful as those three."

It was the most touching thing I have ever heard Sten utter.

chapter 9
Scales of Time, Scales of Truth

Each charter starts with the potential for drama. When the elements and boating are mixed with people fishing, something inevitably jolts life out of the norm. I often mused that that was precisely what people were looking for when they boarded my vessel. There is never anything routine when you take a group of strangers out on the water. Some of the events already chronicled in this book demonstrate how a simple activity like fishing can lead to experiences that stay with you for life. The earth does not have to move with each charter, but quite often it quivers. If you are not in tune with one of the elements, you will miss the interchange. It is not always the *coup de foudre* that is missed but the gentle breeze that turns your sails in the other direction. The lack of predictability is a strong attraction for sport fishermen. (I emphasize sport fishermen, because commercial fishermen have a vastly different agenda.)

I fielded a call on our business line from a couple who wished to charter the boat exclusively for themselves. When I explained they would have to shoulder all the charges, they agreed without hesitation. The following day they arrived punctually. I was a little taken aback when I discovered they were in their eighties.

Over the telephone the man had sounded like a fellow in his early fifties. They came aboard with the enthusiasm of curious fifty-year-olds boarding a pirate ship.

More power to them, I thought, but made a mental note to keep them on the lower deck.

If it isn't already obvious, I have a lot of fun observing people's behaviour. Social, cultural, demographic and education divisions become evident after a few hours of conversation. In one of the cultural boxes is wealth. I have known only one or two wealthy people who came by their affluence through inheritance. Almost all the very prosperous people I've met or taken aboard my boat were those who began life with little in the way of riches and who made their fortunes through their own efforts.

My further observations are that most people with serious wealth place great importance on it. It becomes a way of defining themselves and separating themselves from people whose endeavours have not yielded financial rewards. Their counterparts are people who resent the wealthy. They refer to them with contempt as "the rich" and treat them as a separate, barely human species while they, of course, are "the real people." I'm not referring to the super rich, that group of cocooned people who have inherited their wealth and are willing to spend $50,000 to fly from Seattle to Dubai with no idea that amount of money can be a year's or even two years' salary for some people.

The people I'm referring to are those who have packed away a chunk of change that takes all worry out of life. I like the company of this group and enjoy observing how ease affects them. Many of them will say, quite without affectation, that their wealth merely supports their conviction of their own intellectual or business superiority. Some will tell you how lucky they are and how timing played an important role in their success. It pleases me that very few of these people feel guilty that their good judgment and business acumen brought them financial rewards.

The octogenarians on this charter introduced themselves as Elmer and Violet. From English immigrant families, they carried in their speech remnants of their North Country heritage. Speaking fondly of their parents, they reported with exuberance how much fun and how unencumbered their childhoods had been and what a surprise it was, when in their teens, to discover they were poor. Their background was not one in which alcohol or drugs were needed to deaden their lives. From an early age, they had been taught to work diligently to obtain an education, which would allow them to leap frog, financially, over their parents. Both had found a way to obtain a university degree, and both had developed successful business projects that led to their financial comfort. They understood that the fates had aligned the stars in their favour, since they had a number of friends whose projects had not given them the rewards they sought. With the common sense of English lads and lasses with simple, old-fashioned values, they were pleased with the life they had worked to achieve and aware their "brass" gave them no special privileges in life. Twice during the charter I heard them say, "You can't buy beauty or luck, but it's great to be beautiful and lucky." This was evidently their family mantra; even in their eighties it was obvious they had been a handsome couple in their heyday.

By the time we were at the fishing grounds, I knew their story. Everyone has a story, and theirs was just as engaging as that of the young man I had taken out the previous day. His aspiration was to become a nurse and use his skills in his native West Africa.

Because I have a loose attachment to the UK, I was curious about why the parents of these two octogenarians had moved from northern England to Canada. In hindsight it was obvious. Their fathers had known each other before World War I, and together they had survived the German carnage and the inept leadership of their own officers. After the war they wanted to find a quiet place to live that was not directly affected by the war, a place where they could bring their young brides and raise a family.

The choices were Australia, New Zealand, India or Canada, the four corners of the British Commonwealth. Their fathers decided that once they were decommissioned they would move to the city of Halifax in Canada, joining friends who had already made the move to that fine place. Their plans were altered when in December 1917, the French cargo ship ss *Mont Blanc* detonated, killing two thousand people in the city and wounding nine thousand citizens. Vast portions of the town were flattened. Halifax was said to resemble the battleground of Vimy Ridge, where nearly thirty-six hundred Canadians were killed in April of that year. With Halifax in turmoil they altered their plans, setting their sights on the growing city of Vancouver with its spectacular view of the Coast Mountains and the Strait of Georgia. It was there, in 1919, that the two families set down roots and started a new life with all the energy, optimism and fears immigrants bring with them.

Once we reached the area where we planned to fish, I turned off the engine and gave them a quick lesson in drift fishing. At first they were disappointed—they had imagined we were going to troll—but as soon as we had our first strike they were brimming with enthusiasm. There is nothing like feeling a strike to get your adrenalin pumping. Age plays no part in this response. Age certainly did not dampen the enthusiasm of Elmer and Violet.

Often we take people fishing who simply cannot coordinate their responses to a strike. Sten had a comical routine that imitated inept fishermen striking at a fish. His routine always improved with a sampling of my finest single-malt Scotch whisky. On one memorable occasion, we had a blowhard on board who filled the air with stories of his fishing expeditions off the coast of Florida. He told us of the enormous tarpon he'd caught and the exhausting battle he had bringing it alongside the boat. With this kind of experience, we expected he'd be a cool customer when he struck into a salmon. Nothing could have been further from the truth. When he did have a strike, his response was to drop his rod, shout that he had a fish on and dance around as though a mouse was nipping at his heels. Fortunately Sten was close by and was able to snatch up the rod and play the fish until we persuaded our guest that he could deal with the salmon. Sten had to baby talk him through the entire procedure and reassure him, once the fish was safely netted, that he had done well.

Elmer and Violet were not cut from this cloth. They noticed things before they were pointed out and marvelled at the serenity while drifting with the current. Not unexpectedly they were competitive with each other, but they had no intentions of keeping any of the salmon they hooked and played. Their interest was in the experience.

It was in this manner we drifted past the kelp bed and through Race Passage, sliding over Dr. Cliff's Hole, which produced only the story and legend of Cliff. Elmer and Violet were fascinated with his story and prompted me to elaborate on his character and good luck. They were riveted by the story of his last thirty pounder, and Violet was near tears when I told them how I had learned of his death.

"You must certainly meet some interesting people," Violet remarked.

"Most people have something interesting to tell you if you just take the time to listen."

"Of course, but you have to listen to a lot of blather before you hear something worthwhile," she quipped.

She had me in stitches of laughter because she was right. In so many cases, it is difficult to pick out the nuggets from a sack of trash, and sometimes the nugget is so small it's hardly worth the effort.

Drifting along quietly, we discussed this subject, marvelling at how some people place little value on the extraordinary things they have accomplished, while other people caw like scavenging ravens over their most mundane achievements. I recounted a story about the son of one of my father's friends, who turned up on Dad's doorstep with his backpack. Since he was a family friend, he was invited in, shown to a room and promptly fed. No one passed over my parents' threshold without being fed; I always thought of this as remnant of their days in Kenya. My parents sat with the boy at their kitchen table and listened patiently to the woes of this indolent, apathetic young man who had been brought up with all the advantages of a North American child. An onlooker to this scene, I stood in the doorway and listened to complaint after complaint pouring out of this young fellow. At one point my father half turned his head to me and rolled his eyes with a slight shrug of his shoulders.

Little did this soft North American kid know that sitting beside him was a man who had spent nearly four years behind enemy lines during World War II and had never once complained about that experience. The lad's whining seemed so trivial and so utterly feckless.

Elmer and Violet nodded their heads. They too were constantly appalled by the trivial values exhibited by so many of their acquaintances and their offspring.

"Values of used car salesmen," snorted Violet.

"Trivial people with trivial values," echoed Elmer.

I was pleased to hear the hard edge of their opinion. Most of the time all we hear or read are benign platitudes from mealy-mouthed government speakers or news readers. These two old dears had seen real battle and come through with fully formed opinions from their life experiences. It certainly made conversation lively, even when we disagreed—and we disagreed on a lot of things, from rearing children to religion. Never once did they hold their fire and I felt no compunction to hold mine. I've always found it refreshing to speak my mind without concern of offending someone. They laughed openly at some of my thoughts and I rattled their cages, accusing them of being closed-minded. We had a great time.

To punctuate our conversations we hooked, played and released salmon. This was one of those charters I would remember with pleasure. Great weather, great people and great fishing—my trinity.

Before going in, I suggested we drift past the RON Blasting rock a few times. When I said I hoped we might be able to connect them with a Texas-sized salmon, they were as excited as kids at a carnival. The conditions were ideal for a slow drift past RON Blasting. We were close to high slack tide, the sun was out and a light breeze was keeping us cool. All we needed was a large, silent ghost at the end of our line. Conditions were ideal, so I decided to wet a line and see whether an extra lure in the water would assist matters.

We continued to chat as we fished, solving the problems of the world with a few strokes of our imaginary sceptres. We had fun taking turns creating fictional laws that would end all armed conflict or rectify some of the atrocities of the recent past.

"Wouldn't it be great if we could bring back to life the twelve million Christians killed under the Soviet regime?" Violet asked.

I demurred on this point since I am of the opinion that control of the world population is one of our most important tasks. Mind you, slaughtering twelve million of your own people is not my idea of population control.

Twelve million human beings! The number is beyond comprehension. How numb must a society be to allow such torture to occur? It brought to mind other human catastrophes of recent decades. Elmer reminded us that in 1918, waves of Spanish flu wiped out at least twenty million people worldwide. There was the Armenian genocide, the extraordinary horrors of World War II, Rwanda, the North American Indians, the South American Indians, the Hawaiian people—the list went on. It became too depressing so we changed the subject.

Violet described her great-grandchildren and how brilliant they were but how she deplored the parenting skills of their parents. I reminded her that all generations deplore the parenting of the new generation. She harrumphed at me, suggesting I didn't know what I was saying. Her strong convictions made me smile.

While we were talking, we drifted past the RON Blasting rock for the first time, where the current was setting up a slight back eddy. Sten and I referred to this spot as "the elbow"; occasionally we picked up a nice salmon around this corner. On this day, our first drift produced nothing except good chatter. When we pulled in our lines I promised this lovely couple that our second drift was going to be different. We planned to drift past RON with our stern to the rock and the engine running. Just as we passed the face of the rock, Sten would slip us into reverse and jog us back a few feet. When this was done, they were to lower their lines to the bottom and reel up two cranks—about a foot—then continue to fish as usual.

Sometimes these manoeuvres work. Other times, they are pointless if no one is home or you present the wrong bait. On this occasion I was hopeful; the air smelled of fish and the tide was making the right sound. Yes, fishermen live on hope. Sometimes we change lures or the presentation just to give ourselves hope. It is part of the fun of fishing. On an impulse I changed my lure, attaching an extra-large white Buzz Bomb. It had been in my drawer for a long time but never used because of its size and weight.

Sten positioned us nicely for a stern drift past the rock. The tide created small waves that slapped against our hull and exquisite terns danced over the surface bait. If you observe them closely, you will see them drop over some feed, pick up a herring or needle fish and then turn it with their beak to swallow it straight down. They give a little shudder with their wings as they swallow their food. When I pointed this out to Elmer and Violet, they nearly forgot to lower their lines because they were so enthralled with the terns.

The elderly couple fished over the transom while I dropped my heavy lure over the starboard side close to them. Sten was at the helm, watching the paper sounder and calling out the depth as we drifted past RON.

"Now," he called out as he slipped us into reverse and goosed the engine just enough to move us back slightly. The current caught us and pulled us into the elbow.

I let my lure flutter to the bottom then cranked it up a foot. Elmer and Violet followed suit. There was an air of anticipation; we grinned at each other as we fished. It was almost as though we were listening to a favourite melody with our heads cocked to the ocean. At the apex of my pull I felt a bump, and immediately I let the lure flutter to the bottom before pulling it back up. This time there was a heavy hit, and I struck. The fish was on. Elmer and Violet burst into applause.

"Any size?" Sten asked.

"A slug."

"Gaff or net?"

"I'm not sure yet."

"You going to hand it off?"

"Maybe. But it could be a ling."

Sten stored Elmer and Violet's rods and stood beside me. I could feel the weight of the fish but could not identify it by its behaviour. It was not shaking its head and it was not taking a run. It felt like a dead weight pulling down on my gear.

"You think it's a 'but?"

"Could be."

I half turned to see our octogenarians with linked arms, watching the activities with delight.

"Which of you would like to play this fish?"

As one person they shook their heads. "You play it, Peter," Violet said. "It's just as much fun for us to watch." A twinkle glowed in her eyes as she spoke. Elmer was grinning.

"Are you sure? This is something big."

"Go ahead—you play it. I'll take the pictures," Elmer insisted.

For nearly twenty minutes we drifted away from RON and into the mouth of the bay. The fish never sounded nor did it take a serious run. It seemed to be moving underwater with the drift of our boat. With only fifteen-pound test line, not many mistakes are allowed with a large fish. I was convinced it was a halibut in the forty- to sixty-pound range. It's difficult to tell with a flat fish— they can hold their body against your pull and fool you. Patience is your only ally. Patience and pressure—you have to keep pressure on the fish. That means the pressure is on your arms and shoulders for as long as you play it. This fellow was a "sulker"—it didn't want to run and it didn't want to surface. Sometimes anglers snap metal objects around the line and allow them to slide onto the nose of the fish with the idea of irritating it into activity. Sten and I decided against this manoeuvre. We thought it best just to wait.

The fish never really came to life. I ended up pumping it gradually to the surface. Sten was standing beside me, quivering with excitement. In preparation he was wielding the three-foot handle of a gaff. He was so excited I could hear his teeth chatter.

While I worked the halibut, I answered questions from Elmer and Violet. At one stage, Elmer took the rod from my hand just to get the feel of the pressure. He promptly handed it back to me. "Pleased you're playing that fish and not me," he said.

Gradually I made some gains, retrieving line and forcing the fish closer to the surface. It still made no effort to run or throw the lure. Sten, still vibrating like an Irish setter in pointing stance, had the gaff firmly gripped in his right hand and kept muttering that he wished we had Jim on board with his rusty old rifle.

When the halibut was close enough, Sten reached under the rail and gaffed it. I put down my rod, picked up the second gaff and gaffed it on the other side of the head. Together we slipped the large flat fish onto the stern deck and prepared to immobilize it. Everything was so calm I should have known better.

Halibut are well known for playing possum before exploding into a mad fury. Stories of small boats found with a dead fisherman and a dead halibut lying at the bottom of the boat make the rounds. With its inoffensive teeth, the halibut does not bite; rather, it uses its muscular body to batter its captor.

Our fellow, at nearly sixty pounds, took up a great deal of the stern deck and looked ominous lying there without moving. It seemed as though it was pulsating in thought only.

While Sten turned to reach for the dispatching knife, Elmer stepped closer to the fish to fill the frame of his camera. Fortunately Violet was standing on the top step of the companionway when the fish exploded into action. With a single convulsive move, Elmer was smacked on his calves and knocked on top of the halibut, where he was juggled like a ball on the tip of a seal's nose. The noise was deafening, like an excavator tearing down a house, with Elmer's grunts and exclamations thrown into the mix. If the situation had not been so serious, I would have laughed out loud. It was like something from a French cartoon.

Sten and I jumped on top of the halibut in an effort to smother its movements. Briefly we bounced around like bull riders. Our combined weight allowed Elmer to roll into a corner, where he promptly raised his camera and snapped another set of pictures. With a single stroke of the dispatching knife, Sten killed the fish. Silence hung over the boat for a few seconds before the three of us men started howling with laughter. The image, from on high, must have looked ridiculous. Two grown men perched on top of a halibut, one with a knife in his hand. Beside them was an eighty-year-old man taking pictures while his wife looked on in stunned silence. It was a picture that could have put us all in the loony bin.

Poor old Elmer. When everything returned to normal, I rolled up his pant legs to examine his calves. They were a vivid red and had been terribly smacked. I was sure they would be multicoloured by the following morning. While Sten filleted the fish I made some ice packs, which I secured around Elmer's calves. I knew he was going to be an achy old man the following day.

Violet showed him not an ounce of sympathy. "Silly old fool—what were you thinking? You could have had a broken leg. All for what—a picture of a fish?"

I was reminded of a scene from *The Yearling* but thought it best not to mention it. I knew she was worried.

That halibut was our good fortune. Since Elmer and Violet were travelling, they had no use for any of the fillets. With their blessing Sten and I shared the fish evenly. I took portions of my share to my mum and dad, who gave it a light smoking before baking it and serving it with a white sauce and capers. My son Ian and I froze some of the fillets but cooked most of it while it was still fresh. Freezing takes the bloom off the flavour.

The story of Elmer and Violet has a coda. Two years later I took a nondescript couple out fishing. They were quiet and friendly but not terribly enthusiastic. I had the impression they were not really interested in fishing or the scenery.

Something's going to hatch, I thought.

Sure enough, after three hours of muddling around, they eventually broached the subject that interested them. They asked whether, a few years previously, I had taken out a couple called Violet and Elmer.

Ah! Here it comes. I pulled out the ship's photo album and showed them a picture of Violet and Elmer with their halibut on the deck.

"Did they really catch it?" I was asked.

I looked as awed as I could and confirmed that they had.

"I can't understand how my dad could land such a big fish."

What a thrill to know the trip had been so memorable to Elmer and Violet that their son wanted to share their experience. "It was tricky," I said.

"How long did it take him?"

"A while."

"He said it was about a hundred pounds, but you had to guess because your scales weren't big enough."

Sten and I looked at each other. "One hundred pounds?" I asked.

"At least," he said.

"Hmm . . . that sounds about right," I said, thinking on the fly. "But it's true—we couldn't be sure since my scales don't go up that far."

With that he fumbled in his backpack and produced a splendid set of weighty, solid brass scales with a large circular porcelain dial. They were the Rolls-Royce of scales, beautifully made by a world-famous European firm.

He handed them to me. "My dad wants you to have these. Just to keep you honest."

A hint of a smile played on his face as he spoke.

chapter 10
Young Guests

During the first couple months of operating the charter boat, our friends and relatives booked with us simply to give us the business and to give the impression of activity. At that time, our standard family rate was double price in order to help the new business. Later, when the business was up and rolling, the family rate was free.

Among our friends who booked early on was my father's retired boss, Robin. He lived on the East Coast of the United States, where he was enduring his retirement. Although he had led a successful business life, his family life had been dramatic and difficult. When my father told him about our new venture, he immediately booked three days for himself and his fifteen-year-old grandson Ted, who was his ward. Our booking calendar was sparsely filled, and it was a relief to have three days blocked off.

A few weeks after making the booking, Robin and Ted flew in from the United States and moved into the Oak Bay Beach Hotel, a short walk to my parents' house. I was stunned at how much Robin had aged compared with my father and equally stunned at how much Ted resembled his grandfather. He even showed many of his mannerisms.

It was a treat to have the two old warriors around the same dining room table and to hear of their business struggles as the decanter of port made its rounds. Both these men had started their lives with extraordinary parents but without financial backing. It was riveting to listen to their stories describing how they had successfully worked their way up the corporate ladder to their respective positions of president and vice president. Both these men had actively served in World War II. My father's war years were spent on the Chinese-Vietnamese border, where he accumulated intelligence for the British; Robin was vague when discussing his contribution so I did not press him for details. I did know that both men were highly decorated and neither one of them discussed their awards. I was proud to be in their company although I wasn't sure Ted enjoyed being with the older generation.

Ted was a quiet lad with a friendly smile. He had brought a stack of classical literature to read while in Canada. I am an avid reader, so that was our point of contact. He was reading *Anna Karenina* for the first time and was finding the dense prose a bit daunting. I told him I hadn't read *Anna Karenina* until I was eighteen and like him, I'd struggled with the volume of language and the constant name changes.

Our first two charters with Robin and Ted were a preamble for the third day. In this era of fishing, Sten and I trolled using the standard local gear, which included heavy wooden reels and stiff fibreglass rods. Made of varnished, hand-turned oak with brass fixtures, the reels were aesthetically attractive but cumbersome if you were accustomed to lighter gear. We always thought they were better suited as display items.

In later years we joked that those first two days were part of our catch-and-release program since we played a number of good fish but they all escaped. Ted was feeling particularly despondent; he thought he would never land a salmon and that it would be better if his grandfather played the strikes. We were all there to put wind under his wings and assure him that he was simply living through his learning curve.

When we gathered at 4:00 PM for their last charter, rain clouds had moved in and a stiff breeze was blowing. The windsock was cracking on our light mast and the boat was tugging at its mooring lines. But there was never a question of staying in our slip; we all knew it would take a hurricane to cancel the trip.

We went straight through Race Passage then turned to port with the idea of exploring the fishing at the far side of the lighthouse. While the weather was not dangerous, Robin and Ted had not travelled three thousand miles to experience a dark sky, a stiff breeze and a rapidly changing tide. Robin and my father plunked themselves down at the dinette table and continued to bring each other up-to-date on their activities.

I heard only snippets of their conversation because I was chatting with Ted in an effort to buoy his spirits. He felt depressed. They had travelled such a long distance only to have him lose four nice salmon on the first two charters. He loved his grandpa and wanted to make him proud.

At one point I asked him if he enjoyed fishing and his answer was telling.

"Kinda."

A long silence ensued. Then I asked him whose idea it was to fly to our corner of the world to fish for salmon.

"Grandpa asked me if I wanted to do some fishing in Canada. I didn't know it would be so far away."

"What do you like doing?"

"You know, the usual stuff."

"Like?"

"You know, reading and stuff."

"What other stuff?"

"Stuff like driving."

"Driving?"

"Go-karts and stuff."

"You drive go-karts?"

"Grandpa and me build them, then I drive them."

"Tell me about that. How do you start building a go-kart?"

I am mechanically inclined, so I expected to be awash in technical jargon. But instead of talking about the nuts and bolts of a go-kart, he spoke at length about the joy he felt when working with his grandpa in their converted garage. He told me how his grandpa would give the engine parts Christian names and refer to them by these names. Pivotal parts were named after the Apostles, so his grandpa would say "Pass me Matthew" or "We're now going to put John and Mark together." A lost or misplaced part was named Satan or The Big B. An important or well-made part became Jesus. When they ran short of Christian names, his grandpa would select names from Greek mythology, which he said was much the same stuff as the mythology from the New Testament.

Listening to him talk, I easily observed that the boy and his grandfather were very close. He didn't mention his parents and his relationship with them, so I didn't ask. There was clearly a deep story running through this young man, who was far too collected for a North American lad his age.

While these conversations were going on, Sten trolled our lines parallel to the lighthouse. As Ted talked, we made several passes down our side of the lighthouse then looped around to repeat the pass. I kept an eye on the lines and cleared them of pieces of kelp. The bells on the downriggers remained silent, so we decided to troll into Race Passage to catch the change of tide.

The tide change can be dramatic in Race Passage, as we were to learn with many charters in subsequent years. Just before making our turn into the channel, the starboard bell rang. It was a hard, sharp ring that usually indicated a nice salmon had taken the lure and popped the line off the downrigger cable. I snatched up the rod and reeled in the slack line. As soon as I made contact with the fish I handed the rod to Ted, who was waiting beside me. The sound of the bell brought my father and Robin on deck. Dad watched the communication between Sten and me. I held up ten fingers then seven, and Sten showed thumbs-up and nodded his head.

While the second downrigger was brought in, Sten took us past the rocks and into Race Passage, where he throttled back as much as he could.

For a young man worried about pleasing his grandpa, Ted was as cool as a jade egg. The past two charters had taught him to keep his rod tip up, to palm his reel when the salmon was taking a run, and to keep his fingers away from the whirling handles. He had learned from his previous losses and could now anticipate the actions of the fish. He needed little coaching; skilfully, he allowed the line to be taken out by the salmon before smoothly reeling it back in.

At one point the flood and ebb tide met each other twenty feet from the stern of our boat. They slid past each other like shifting tectonic plates. For a magical minute, we could see Ted's salmon swimming in the curling wave of the incoming water. It was akin to watching it through the glass of a life-sized aquarium. We saw it swim from left to right then turn and retrace its path before diving straight down and running out over a hundred feet of line. You would have to fish ten thousand days to see that sight again.

"Awesome!" said Ted as a round of applause erupted.

Moments like these make up the puzzle pieces of who we are. I wanted to hug Ted for being moved by the sight of the salmon in the waves. My father, Robin, Sten and I all nodded to one another with huge smiles on our faces. Robin was tearing up, his mouth working furiously to disguise the feelings that had just flooded over him. My dad put his hand on the back of his friend's neck and gave him a gentle squeeze; Robin nodded but continued to struggle with his weepy eyes.

The only time I had to give Ted instructions was when it was time to net his fish. He was very excited, and my job was to talk him through the last stages of playing this salmon.

"Bring him in closer, but keep his head just under water." A lot of fishermen make the mistake of trying to lift their salmon out of the water instead of allowing it to slide into the basket of the net. Ted was in direct accord with me. He brought his fish close to the surface then directed it into the net. I pulled up on the handle, locked the fish into the basket and swung it onto the deck.

Grandpa Robin wrapped his arms around his grandson and gave him a big hug and a kiss. He was streaming tears; we on the outside of this drama clapped some more and congratulated the young lad. Ted could not take his eyes off the salmon. It was a magnificent specimen. Long and clean, without any sea lice, it was a beautiful gift from the ocean.

I looked up at Sten, who was beaming at the helm. "It's gotta go seventeen," I said.

"Twenty by tomorrow," he answered.

I nodded toward Race Passage, and Sten turned back to the helm and started us toward the dock. There was still enough light for another hour of fishing, but I thought it best to go in on a successful note and while the weather was acceptable.

After we had cleared Race Passage and made the turn into the bay, Sten signalled to me that he needed a break before preparing the salmon. When I took the helm, the grandfathers were at the dinette table and Ted was examining his salmon. Relief washed over me that we had found the young lad a lovely fish and that he'd landed it using the skills developed over the past few days. I loved to be at the helm, sliding over the water following a successful day of fishing. Sometimes I played Jean-Pierre Rampal tapes as we made our way to home port until Sten would tell me to change the music. He was convinced many of our guests found Rampal's music annoying. For some reason, on this occasion I thought the music would be suitable, so I slipped in an old tape and turned the knob that opened the speakers in the galley.

Within a few minutes Ted was at my side. "Do you like flute music?" he asked.

"Yes, but not all of it."

"We think Rampal is great!"

Here was another surprise from this young man. I knew few boys his age who could tolerate a flute playing classical music. "I have one of his tapes where he plays Gaelic music," I said. "Would you like me to put that one on?"

"This one's fine. Grandpa has most of his stuff. We play it all the time in the workshop."

"While you're looking for Matthew, Mark, Luke and John?"

For the first time, since I had met him, Ted broke into full laughter, exposing the wire braces in his mouth and making his eyes disappear into tiny slits. For that short moment, he was a young boy caught in the image of his own humour.

"This has been so cool. Thanks for taking us out."

"It's been our pleasure." As an afterthought, I added, "Would you like to take the helm?"

It was as though someone had put his fingers in an electric socket. "Could I?" His voice rose and cracked; his cool disappeared.

"Sure, go ahead—take the helm. And keep us on that compass course." I indicated the eight-inch liquid compass directly in front of him. Stepping aside, I let him stand in front of the wheel.

A grin emerged that stretched from one side of his face to the other. He was the image of pure joy. "This is so cool."

"Better than fishing?"

"Kind of."

"Like driving a go-kart?"

"Yeah, just like that but heavier."

On our way in, I had him take us twice around the Navy Can buoy on full plane. A fifty-foot, seventeen-ton vessel skipping over the water on full plane and turning in a tight circle is a lot of fun, and it was sheer joy to young Ted. A massive grin was locked on his face even when we disembarked at the dock.

The following day when we took them to the Victoria International Airport, Ted gave me a brief, self-conscious hug. "That was neat. Thanks, Mr. Gordon."

I knew he was not talking about the fishing.

* * *

On another charter we took out an unaccompanied eleven-year-old boy. In today's cultural climate I would probably decline the booking, but at the time I did not hesitate. My children had flown unaccompanied for years and I had done the same when I was their age.

Chad lived in the Northwest Territories and was visiting his grandparents in Victoria. They both had hip problems but wanted their grandson to have a fishing experience. Without questioning them, I gave them a list of things the boy should bring on board and told them to deliver him to the boat a little ahead of schedule so we would have time to get to know each other. On the day of the charter he arrived half an hour early, and in only ten minutes he had explored every corner of the *Kalua* and knew where the restricted areas were.

Prior to meeting him, I imagined he would be an active, wiry boy perhaps a little on the shy side. He turned out to be tall for his age and quite tubby with pale skin, flaming red cheeks and copper-coloured hair. He was alert and enthusiastic, peppering us with questions about fishing. He wanted to know all about the electric cables that connected us to the shore and how we had hot water in the sink. I love inquisitive kids, especially when they ask surprising questions. For the duration of the charter, Sten and I were kept on our toes answering questions and explaining how things worked.

After the other guests arrived we cast off, and with Chad sitting beside Sten at the helm, we made our way to the fishing grounds. It was the second week of August, so we had a good chance of catching salmon ranging from five to forty pounds. We had the light spinning gear out with everyone fishing with fresh fifteen-pound test line. This was not one of those charters during which we could only hope to catch a fish; today, we *knew* we were going to do well. These were the charters that sustained us when the fishing was slow.

Chad posed no problem. I found him a good spot where he could easily work his rod and told him to take a break every half hour. I reminded him to use plenty of sunblock and to wash his hands after applying it. Both Sten and I kept an eye on him, which proved to be unnecessary since he was a well-behaved young lad who laughed easily. The other guests made sure to include him in their activities and invited him to join them when they pulled out their picnic lunches. To his credit, he pulled out the pack lunch his grandparents had made for him and shared it with the other people. One thing I had forgotten about children was how much they had to pee. At first I thought he simply liked to work the elaborate mechanism in the head, but he assured me this was normal for him. To be on the safe side, I kept him well hydrated with spring water from the ship's tank.

When we started to catch fish, Chad always reeled in his line and somehow found his way next to the fisherman playing the fish. He was never exactly in the way but he was certainly present. Once the fish was netted, he beetled back to his rod and fished again with renewed enthusiasm. More than anything he wanted to take a salmon back to his grandparents, who had filled his head with mythical stories of giant chinook.

The inevitable occurred. Two hours into the charter, Chad screamed. It is a delight to hear surprise and excitement all in one sound. Without waiting, Chad's salmon streaked away, heading straight out to sea. He could barely hold onto his rod because the drag was synched down. Sten, close to him, loosened it slightly and walked Chad to the stern of the boat with his hands on the boy's shoulders. The rest of the fishermen reeled in their lines.

The salmon ran straight out before swinging slightly to the right. In the flick of an eye it was charging back toward the boat like a torpedo. For nearly thirty seconds we had no contact with the fish as Chad reeled in the slack line and we repositioned him at the other side of the stern. When he did make contact, the fish had gone under the boat and was streaming out line as it raced into the bay. I didn't like to do it, but I took the rod out of his hands. I dipped the tip as far under water as I could, then walked around the transom and worked the line past the stationary propeller. When I cleared the propeller, I gave the rod back to Chad on the other side of the boat.

This was a crazy, hyperactive salmon. One minute it was on its way to Port Angeles, and the next it was sounding and unwrapping yards of line from the reel. Chad was almost a bystander, alternately allowing line to run out and reeling it in as quickly as he could. I didn't know who was going to wear out first, Chad or his salmon. After over twenty-five anxious minutes, the line went dead. One second the rod was buzzing out line, and the next minute there was no activity at all. There was weight at the other end, but it was a dead weight—more like a clump of kelp. With heavy disappointment I told Chad to reel in his line so we could see what was at the other end. While he was reeling in, he kept saying something was on his hook but it was not moving.

"Reel, and let's take a look," I urged.

To everyone's surprise the lump of kelp we'd imagined proved to be his salmon. It was floating on its side, completely exhausted. The wild runs had taken their toll. With no fanfare Sten dipped the net in the ocean and brought the fish on board. There was a round of applause for the grinning little boy, who kept saying, "The grands are going to go nuts."

Indeed they did. They sent a picture of their grandson, who could barely hold up his twenty-three-pound chinook, to the *Times Colonist*. Chad's story was run on the sports page. He was even awarded a King Fisherman Silver Anniversary decal from the newspaper.

That Christmas, I received a card from Chad's grandparents that included a picture of Chad with his salmon. Along with the card was an appreciative note telling me he had taken the whole salmon back to his parents in the Northwest Territories.

* * *

After a couple of years of operation, Magna Charters was a well-known entity in the tourist industry in Victoria. The benefit of this notoriety was the local business we attracted. My policy was to offer a 50 percent discount to all local businesses that used our services for their annual office outing. The second year I offered this discount, I thought it might have been a mistake. We had nearly twenty companies take us up on our offer, which created a serious reduction in our cash flow. However, the benefit came in subsequent years when the people who had been out on these junkets had visitors in town they wished to entertain.

One day, I answered a message on the company answering machine. I thought I recognized the voice but was not certain. In parts of Ireland they speak English in soft, quiet tones, almost a whisper. The message was in this dialect of English. When I eventually made contact with the caller, he turned out to be an acquaintance who had a thriving antique store in Victoria. A branch of his family was coming over from Ireland and he wanted to take them all, including the wives and kids, for an afternoon cruise. Fishing was not the primary objective.

I made the booking, reminding him to have his family bring rain gear and baskets of food since we didn't provide food or beverages on discounted charters. He made a few disparaging remarks about how tightly Scots kept their purse strings pulled and promised to be on time. I suggested that an Irishman promising anything was as useful as a toad in a teapot. I knew this was going to be a fun charter. The idea of taking out a family straight off the plane from Ireland had me laughing with anticipation. There would be no slithering political correctness or bureaucratic double talk on this charter. I could hardly wait.

To no one's surprise, they were late. Irish Time is a time unto itself. Anticipating their tardiness, we had not turned on the engine until we saw them starting down the ramp to the dock. I had been told there would be six of them but we counted eight as they approached—three men and their wives and two young boys, Aedan and Cian. Despite being late, I knew they were a great group from the outset. Open and gregarious, they marvelled at unfamiliar things and scoffed at familiar things. I bundled them all into the forward cabin, where they stored their spare clothes and baskets of food.

In my briefing on our proposed course and the few rules aboard the *Kalua*, I began by referring to their host Brian as Brian Boru, a former high king of Ireland. This broke them into peals of laughter with much back slapping of Brian's septuagenarian shoulders. We never looked back from that moment, and for the remainder of the trip everyone was boisterous and friendly. While they did bring their own poteen, no one was difficult or misbehaved. As a group they had some difficulty understanding why neither Sten nor I would imbibe a drop of their nectar.

While the sun was not blazing, the day was fresh without being cold and there was little wind. To this group from Ireland it was perfect weather. We cruised along the coast then went out into the straits to have a closer look at the snow-capped Olympic Range that floated in the distance. We turned off the engine and drifted with the current while everyone tucked into their picnic. It was solid food, unlike the gourmet treats our restaurateurs from San Francisco had carried in their hampers. I had a side of gravlax, which I carved into thin slices with my long, exquisite carving knife. Sometimes, with extra-nice people, we made exceptions to our rule about not feeding the guests, and I happily passed around portions for this pleasant group to taste. With the rest, Sten and I made sandwiches with dill sauce and lettuce.

"Not bad for a Canadian Pacific salmon but not a patch on smoked Irish Atlantic salmon," one of them taunted.

It was all good-natured banter. For something that was "not bad," they managed to scarf down the entire side of gravlax by the end of the charter. When I told my father how much they had enjoyed it he was delighted. Both of us had been recipients of kindness on our numerous visits to Ireland. It was nice to be able to return the favour.

While we were cruising around, a pod of orcas travelled past us, going in the opposite direction. I could not have staged a more dramatic sight. While the adults slipped past us, two of the youngsters in the pod rolled and breached as they went by. It is difficult to describe the glory of seeing these splendid cetaceans in the ocean. They exude a wondrous sense of freedom in the vast waters that are their home. Once you have seen them free, travelling by their own compass in the open ocean, it horrifies you that aquariums and other hucksters put them on display in tanks of water so they can charge the general public to see them. I have no kind words for these people, even if they do produce modest insights into cetacean behaviours. Not all things need to be poked, prodded and examined for the benefit of human knowledge. Anything they do to these wonderful mammals they should be willing to do to their own children.

We watched the orcas until even my binoculars could not pick them out. Then we reluctantly headed back to the bay. I wanted to be moored within the hour but there was still time to break out some rods; the younger members of the group were interested in trying some fishing. I ran the idea by the venerable Brian Boru and he agreed.

Sten picked out a tide line and set us adrift in it with the engine off. After giving a brief lecture on how to drift fish and how to handle our fishing gear, I stationed the two youngest members at the stern of the boat. The adults were happy to sit around, chat and sip their spirits. We were losing light, but it was a soft evening with only a light breeze that brought us the smell of the sea. Everyone spoke in quiet tones, admiring the sight of the mountains in the distance and the black and white lighthouse of Race Rocks. It was an excellent opportunity for me to rub in the fact that the lighthouse had been built in 1860 out of Scottish granite that had been brought over expressly to build the main tower. Brian Boru had nothing to say about this fact. He did wonder aloud if we were fishing in vain as he was not sure a Scot could find a salmon in a fish market.

"It's a mug's game," said the mother of the young lads. "Fishing is a mug's game," she repeated.

None of this deterred Aedan and Cian. I approached Aedan, the eldest boy, and asked how he was doing. He was concerned that he was not working the lure properly so I gave him another quick lesson, demonstrating the technique.

"They usually take it when it's fluttering down, so be prepared when you bring your rod tip up. Be prepared to strike."

The wonderful thing about the young is their enthusiasm. Each boy was positive it was only a question of time before he would have a strike. I was not quite as optimistic but, like most fishermen, I figured as long as a line was in the water there was a chance for a fish.

The surprise of a strike is the magic of fishing. I was talking to Cian when a muffled grunt came from my left. It is a universal sound heard around the world. When I looked at Aedan, his whippy little rod was doubled over and line was spooling from his reel in short jerks. He was peering overboard, where his line disappeared into the ocean.

"It's heavy" was all he could manage.

I checked his drag then told him to relax and stand up straight. The rod would do the rest. As I finished speaking, the salmon decided to make a run. Aedan's reel screamed as the line was drawn out at high speed. The sound of his reel had everyone rushing to the stern of the boat.

"Aren't you always the lucky one," Cian said. There was only envy, not spite, in his tone; it was a younger brother chiding the good fortune of an older brother. I had no time to smooth his feathers.

Aedan had obviously fished before. He was now standing straight with his rod pointed up as the line streamed off his spool. As I stood beside him, he glanced over at me.

"How much line do you have on this reel?"

"Enough."

"You sure?"

"He's going to turn soon, so be prepared to reel like crazy."

The fish stopped its run and thrashed in the water, trying to throw the lure. The bouncing at the end of the rod was uneven instead of the smooth feel when the fish was running.

"What's he doing?"

"Trying to throw the hook. Try to move your rod in rhythm with his thrashing." No sooner had I spoken than the salmon decided to make a run back at us, just slightly astern of the boat. "Reel!"

The lad was already reeling, bringing in line as quickly as he could at nearly the same pace as the salmon was swimming toward us. Just as Aedan caught up to the fish it sounded, diving straight down and trailing loose line behind it. Aedan reeled furiously, grunting and puffing as he did. A ring of spectators stood around him, cheering him on and throwing in the occasional word of advice.

Directly astern of us, about twenty feet down, the fish decided to sulk. It swam from side to side at our stern but refused to be raised. I had instructed Aedan in how to pump his rod, but his fish would not yield an inch. It was as though it was holding on to something and would not let go. This presented a couple of problems, the most pressing of which was the fish tearing the hook out. We had not seen whether it was well taken and had no idea whether the hook was coming free. We did not even know whether the salmon had frayed the line or worn the knot.

I decided to let the fish make up its mind but to keep pressure on it. I reached over and tightened the drag a fraction, asking Aedan to keep his rod bowed and to crank in any line the fish gave back.

For several minutes there was little activity. A couple of feet of line were retrieved but the fish would not be moved.

"See if you can pick up some line by dropping your rod tip and reeling. There's no rush—just see if you can move him."

Aedan dropped his rod tip to the surface of the water and reeled in as he did so. Slowly he brought his rod tip up and with it came the fish. He repeated the action. This time it was easier. Each time his rod tip came up Aedan retrieved several feet of line.

Sten was suddenly standing beside me with the landing net. "He's doing good."

"You said it. Let's see if we can get it on the first pass," I replied.

Aedan was very serious, concentrating on working his rod and reel to bring the salmon up and to the boat. At one point he got his first glimpse of it. "It's God himself," he said in reverent awe.

I could see his salmon eight feet below the surface. It had a follower. Sometimes a salmon with a lure in its mouth will draw the company of another salmon curious about the lure.

"Just keep doing what you're doing. See if you can bring it alongside so Sten can reach it with the net."

As good as gold, Aedan eased his fish close to the surface and guided it to the net. In a single clean movement Sten netted the fish and swung it on board.

The entire boat broke into a loud cheer. Young Aedan nearly had the wind knocked out of him from all the pats on his back, and his tired right hand was almost shaken off.

Cian gave his older brother a huge hug. "I nearly died thinking you might lose it."

Pulling out our trusty scales, Sten weighed the fish. It was an even fifteen pounds. A fifteen-pound salmon taken on a light spinning rod with fifteen-pound test line. It does not get any better than that.

chapter 11

The Good and the Bad Among Us

When the oil industry was booming in Alberta and everyone from drilling-mud suppliers to rig suppliers was making preposterous sums of money, Magna Charters benefited. With a little judicious advertising in the right places, we attracted all levels of business from the thriving oil industry. Crews on leave came out with us as well as management courting clients. One of our regular guests was Tahir, who had worked his way up through the system and was the owner of a medium-sized company that supplied essential parts to oil rigs. He was one of those straight-talking people with no time for euphemistic, circuitous, overly loquacious language.

Weather can decide everything. On the day of one of Tahir's charters, the weather was fierce. We were astonished when he turned up for his charter before the crack of dawn with a line of people trailing behind him. A thirty-knot wind was whistling out to sea and an unusual groundswell was rolling symmetrical waves into the bay and through the narrow channel to our moorage. The boat was on loose lines to allow for the wave action along with the rise and fall caused by the groundswell. The dock was bouncing around like a parquet floor in an earthquake. Needless to say, the engine had not even been warmed since I had not seriously considered taking this group out in these conditions.

When Tahir walked to our slip, it was ominously dark and the wind was tearing the words away from his mouth. Only the occasional sound penetrated my hearing as he shouted at me. I went to the stern, pulling the boat closer to the dock so he could clamber on board. Once below deck where we could talk, I said I had no intention of taking his guests into the bay since they would probably be seasick in short order and it would be pointless trying to fish. To make the situation even more dangerous, I was alone on this charter. I can't recall why Sten wasn't along that day.

Disappointed, he tried to negotiate an alternative to the cancellation. "How about my group comes aboard for coffee and to admire the bright work on the *Kalua*?" he asked. He kept combing his wind-tousled hair with a neon green comb while he pleaded with me.

I decided his suggestion couldn't hurt, and without too much trouble I loaded everyone and passed around some fortified coffee. I explained that the weather in the bay was not conducive to fishing—it would be a pointless exercise. Ever the optimist, Tahir asked how long it was expected to last. I couldn't give him an accurate answer. He asked if they could sit around for a while and play some cribbage. I had no objections but made sure he knew the foul weather was likely expected to last through the day. Since they were also booked for the following morning, there was concern their second charter might be cancelled too. I couldn't offer them any hope. My only guarantee was that there was no guarantee.

Two hours later they were still playing cribbage. Stacks of cash were piled around the table, but Tahir was becoming impatient and kept asking me if the wind had slackened.

"Things aren't going to change for a while," I said, "so why don't you pack up your stuff and go back to your hotel and we'll start fresh tomorrow?"

For what must have been the tenth time, he suggested we take a peek around the corner to see what it was like in the bay. In an effort to put an end to their hopes and send them back to their hotel, I said I would cast off and take them into the bay, but he had to understand that as soon as we were free of the dock he had to pay for the full charter. To my amazement he agreed. Sometimes people with too much money say or do stupid things. Talk about calling my bluff! To make sure everyone agreed, I went through the entire group and asked each person whether they wanted to cast off. To my consternation, everyone was in favour, so to impress the conditions on them and, I suppose, to intimidate them, I insisted everyone wear a life jacket. That dampened all their optimistic talk.

I warmed up the engine and cast off. The following wind pushed us through the channel to the black spar-shaped buoy, where I swung us to port and into the bay. I ordered everyone on deck. I did not want people becoming sick below.

A collective gasp went up from the entire group as soon as they caught sight of the bay. Huge rolling waves were coming at us. In the relatively shallow water near the spar buoy the wave action was abrupt, but out in the bay the water built as it undulated up to the ten-fathom mark. To teach this group a lesson, I took the first wave straight on. In spite of all my added ballast, the bow snapped up, and for the very briefest moment it was clear of the water. The wave rolled under us, lifting the stern and sliding us down the other side. In the trough I spun the wheel to port so we would quarter the next wave and goosed the engine to move the stern around. We climbed the second wave to its crest, then I throttled down to allow us to slide down the wave and cut through the crest of the next wave at a quarter angle.

All the guests were hanging on to whatever unmoving ob-ject they could find. No one looked happy. I could already smell bile. To add to their grief, I asked those people close at hand if they would like me to cook them some fried eggs and bacon. Maliciously, I mentioned there were a couple of slices of pepper-oni pizza in the icebox and they were free to help themselves. To add insult to injury, I told them there might also be some cold spaghetti in tomato sauce next to the pizza. No one was amused.

After less than ten minutes of riding the swells, Tahir made his way up the companionway to the helm. He was in a cold sweat.

I grinned at him. "Great, isn't it? Isn't it wonderful to see nature at work?" From his look, I think he would gladly have garrotted me.

"Better go back," he said. "Some of the guys aren't feeling so good."

"Don't worry about that—they'll get over it. Now that we're out here, why don't we stick around?" I was sure that if he'd had a weapon he would have used it.

"Cut it out. Let's go in."

"It's not that easy," I said. "The waves are coming in runs of seven, meaning we'll have to wait for the right moment to make our turn."

I quartered all the waves as they came at us and throttled back so we were making way but not carving through the water. The turn was going to be tricky but exciting. I waited patiently for the right moment. When I saw my chance, I made the turn, and it worked perfectly. One moment we were heading into the bay, and the next we were heading back to the spar buoy and the waves were washing under us. Mooring might be equally tricky. Throughout all this, I was too preoccupied to be afraid. With me, fear invariably comes later.

As we made our way through the channel to our moorage, I called ahead and asked for some assistance at the dock. By the time I was ready to moor, two men were standing on the dock, waiting to grab our lines. As things turned out, the wind slacked off briefly as we came alongside our slip and we were able to tie the boat down without any trouble.

The wind was still bouncing the dock around and our multicoloured windsock was cracking above us. A sorry crew disembarked without one single cheery farewell. Not even when I offered them scrambled eggs and fortified coffee.

Tahir said he would call me at three the next morning to see if they should come out to the marina. He left a fat cheque on the dinette table with a few words scribbled on the back of his business card. He was not a man to use expletives, but in this case he had made an exception.

The following day we were able to cast off without trepidation. While I won't suggest the ocean was glassy and the wind inactive, conditions were tolerable and they were a willing crew.

Sometimes part of the fishing experience for the guests is to handle the fishing gear themselves. When you're trolling, that can be an act of faith since a lot of things can go wrong. Of particular concern are hooks flying around in the wind when the gear is brought in. While no one has ever been badly hooked on my charters, I've had some close calls when clothing or caps were caught.

On this trip everyone knew how to handle the trolling gear and wanted to do all the fishing themselves. This put me in the role of supervisor, chiding them when they tried to take short-cuts and praising them when they performed well.

The water in the bay was still lumpy, but with a collaborative group, full of cheer and optimism, it was fun to be out fishing. As a bonus, no one was seasick. I even cooked them the scrambled eggs I had offered the previous morning—and they ate them with gusto and some fortified coffee.

We trolled up and down the ten-fathom line in the bay and around the kelp bed, but we produced no fish until we ventured out into more open waters. The heaviest fish was just under twenty pounds and the smallest was eight. The gear we were using was local issue. The reels were made of wood with brass fixtures and must have weighed over two pounds each; the rods were thick fibreglass, stiff enough to play a marlin. Today, light-weight world-class single-action reels are made on Vancouver Island and sold around the world. In my charter days, we had to go to Japan to find suitable lightweight quality reels that were simple enough to repair on board.

This group was accustomed to heavy gear so they had no complaints, but bringing in a beautiful eight-pound salmon on this tackle irked me because it took away the finesse of fishing. The highlight of this trip came when we trolled a little too close to the rocks of the lighthouse. The in-line plug, which attaches the fishing line to the downrigger cable, popped free. Because of our location I was sure a cod had caused it. As the fisherman was cranking in his line and mumbling about the drag at the other end, the rod bent over sharply. After a few heavy thumps, the fisherman was able to continue cranking in the line, although with some difficulty. I picked up the gaff and stood beside him, not completely convinced he had not snagged some bull kelp. Slowly the line came in with more thumps along the way. Everyone was speculating. Some thought it was a halibut, while others thought it might be a dogfish. No one was sure enough to place a bet.

Just then, four feet below the surface, I saw a fair-sized black bass held firmly in the prehistoric jaws of a large ling cod.

"Stop reeling!" I grabbed his line in my left hand and slowly raised the ling cod, which was still clamped onto the bass.

Just before the cod broke the surface, I gaffed it and pulled the forty-pound reptilian-looking fish onto the deck. It was a perfect two-for-one catch. Both fish made for a feast.

There is not a ling cod in the world that will ever win a beauty contest. The species has an oversized head with an oversized mouth and a body that tapers to a tail. The skin is mottled and slimy instead of scaly. They have no redeeming physical beauty, but they make succulent fillets and there is very little waste on their skeletons. The guests on this charter were appalled at the sight of this fish, and they were further repulsed when I separated the fillets from the skeleton and they saw that the flesh was green. I could say nothing to convince them that the meat was delicious, so it went on ice and I took it home to share with my parents and my son Ian. I must add that not all ling cod have green flesh—most of the time it is white.

On our way in everyone wanted their picture taken with the huge head of the ling cod with its ugly mouth full of teeth. When they were finished their photo session, I stowed the head and skeleton on ice and used it as bait in my crab pot the following day. When the pot was pulled, it contained five legal Dungeness crabs.

* * *

Not all dramatic events occur when bad weather is swirling around you. Benign weather can lull you into complacency, which in turn can cause silly events to occur.

On one occasion we had aboard a group that included a drama queen. She was out fishing to please her husband but made it abundantly clear he was going to pay dearly for this concession. Sten had identified her as a problem the second she allowed us to help her on board. He was glued to the helm and refused to move.

The weather was flawless for a late-afternoon cruise. With the tide easing into the inlet, our only real concern was from the reflected sunlight. Sten and I smeared sunblock on our faces and forearms and suggested everyone follow suit. There was a general murmur of assent from everyone except our aging diva. In a forceful voice we were told that on no account would she seal her pores with vile, cancer-causing lotion. She further stressed that her body had to breathe at all times but that she would wear her hat—a wide-brimmed toreador affair—and designer sunglasses. I looked at her meticulously applied artificial fingernails and wondered what else was artificial about her, but I simply smiled.

Ms. Wonderful had also come aboard wearing high heels. I suggested she change into something more conventional to avoid doing damage to the *Kalua*'s wooden deck.

"Impossible," she stated, tilting up her head. "High heels are part of my personality and I will not change my personality for anyone." Self-importantly, she squared her body to me and bored her eyes into mine as she spoke. She had obviously taken Assertiveness 101 and 102. It looked as though she was executing a rehearsed move.

Keeping the smile on my face, I said in a quiet voice that as long as she was wearing heels she was confined to the lower deck, the galley and the forward cabin. That didn't faze her.

"We're paying the bill so I'll go where I want."

"If you don't comply, we will not leave the dock," I replied smoothly. A frozen silence cut the air. Everyone stared at me in stunned immobility. Sten was at the helm, looking forward and shaking with mirth. I turned to her husband, adding, "There is no compromise."

Completely at a loss, he looked at some of his friends, but they offered no solution. "Couldn't you make one exception? She always wears heels," he minced.

I was almost grinding my teeth. He was asking me to allow his wife to walk over my decks in high heels, which would damage and leave permanent marks on the smooth finish. I had no idea what would happen if we encountered choppy water and she fell off her heels and sprained an ankle. These kinds of people would surely bring a lawsuit. Again there was a glacial silence.

"I can book you on another charter boat about five miles from here," I offered.

More bewildered silence. Our diva was staring at me with a killer look. I contained my frustration and continued smiling.

"No," said her husband. "You came highly recommended. We want to go out with you." I could see he was looking for wiggle room. He was trying to make nice. I recall thinking any wiggling would have to be done by them. I wasn't going to have my decks ruined just so his wife could wear stilettos on a fishing trip.

"It's easy, folks. Heels off, we go fishing. Heels on, I find you another charter boat."

Without another word the heels came off, but the diva's husband was the target of a deadly look. *Death in the bedroom*, I thought.

Sten threw a look my way. With a subtle gesture, he drew an index finger across his throat. I nodded. This was going to be difficult. There and then, I decided we would not extend the charter as we sometimes did and that while we would remain courteous, we would keep things businesslike.

"Sten, have us moored by eight o'clock sharp." I addressed the group. "Sten will keep us on course and on time." I had a passing thought that if I were a restaurateur I would spit in their soup. My facial muscles were beginning to feel sore from all the forced smiling.

We cruised past the abandoned cement factory to a small, rocky island where we planned to drift fish. The previous day we'd had a lot of action in this location, so I was confident events would repeat themselves within an hour or so.

The conditions were perfect for a wonderful evening of fishing. The tide was easing in slowly, the sun was still warm and we started catching seven- to ten-pound salmon as soon as we put a line in the water.

Ms. Wonderful remained the irritant. Single-handedly, she managed to destroy the pleasant calm of an evening of fishing. Sten was the only one who stayed reasonably impassive, but sometimes he couldn't help himself. At times I would shoot a surreptitious glance his way, and he would mouth some of the inane demands our diva made. It was juvenile, but it kept some levity between us. He lost his composure only once when the diva snapped her fingers at him and abruptly demanded a cold drink in a cold glass. I had to intervene instantly or the Cardinal might have made an appearance. I stepped in between their lines of sight, telling her that I would be pleased to bring her a cold drink in a cold glass, but she was never again to snap her fingers at any of my staff.

A slow smile curled up the corners of her mouth. "Sensitive, is he?" she oozed.

I said as coolly as I could manage, "From now on if you need anything, ask me or your husband. Sten's job today is to keep us on course and on time." I knew she would have to have the last word, but at least it would be with me and not Sten.

"What? Is he the dummy in the group?"

I very nearly smacked her. It was close. I even saw the moment of recognition in her eyes when she realized she'd made a mistake and the look of relief when she knew I was not going to hit her. I had seen that look before and recognized her as a coward; she was strong only when she was immune to any direct retaliation. It bothers me to this day that I didn't say more, but if

I had engaged her in an exchange, pandemonium would surely have broken out.

"People like you never get it" was the best I could do. I was approaching that tipping point where either I endured their company for the next few hours or I called the whole cruise off right then. I went directly below and up the four steps to the helm where Sten was sitting.

"Your call, buddy. Do you want to pull the plug on this charter?" I said this in a loud voice so everyone aboard could hear me. "I'd be pleased to go in. Just say the word."

Sten was positively gleeful. His eyes were dancing and his smile broke open the lower half of his face. "Hell no," he said equally loudly. "Let's see how much fun we can have with these fools."

"You sure?"

"Sure as hell."

I got the soft drink, poured it into a glass and went up the companionway to the rear deck.

Taking the drink, the diva gestured at Sten and said, "What's wrong with him?"

"He gets cranky when he's constipated."

Her husband guffawed, shook his head and smiled. I was at the point of not caring and he seemed to understand this. "I think these fellas wanna take us back to the dock," he said.

She looked surprised. "What's the problem?"

That was the problem—she simply did not get it and probably never would. What I really wanted to do was toss our diva and her spineless husband overboard and get on with life.

I decided to try enduring them. "Have you ever caught a salmon?" I asked her with as much sunshine as I could muster.

"That's his hobby," she said, pointing with her thumb at her husband.

"Why should he have all the fun? I'll show you how, if the salmon will cooperate."

I selected a light trout rod and checked the lure. Just to put on a bit of a show, I pulled out a file and sharpened the hooks. I then demonstrated to her how sharp they were by hanging the lure from my thumbnail. "This is what we call sticky sharp. It's so sharp that even if a salmon flicks it with its tail the salmon will be hooked."

She examined the treble hook and tested each barb on her artificial nails. "Impressive," she conceded.

"Now let's get you down to a depth where you'll have the best chance of catching a salmon." I stripped out the appropriate amount of line while counting aloud. Being physically close to this woman was difficult. She reeked of pharmaceuticals. Her scent was made up of some type of hair product along with her makeup, perfume and what I imagined to be hand cream. She also emanated a light sulphurous odour that I couldn't identify. I gently moved her to the stern of the deck, suggesting she might be comfortable sitting on the transom as she fished.

There is a mystical quality to hooking a fish. As I observe a guest playing a salmon, the odds seem enormous of connecting someone who has travelled all the way from South Africa or some other distant place with a salmon in Canada. I watch the fisherman holding his rod with the line going straight down to sixty or eighty feet and wonder how the fates arranged the meeting. It is a riveting sight—the rigid energy of the fisherman holding a tense, bowed rod and the nearly invisible line stretching deep into the ocean with a salmon at the end battling for its life. It is an ageless story experienced around the world in rivers, lakes and oceans.

This story played itself out with our diva. One moment she was demanding, petulant, self-absorbed and plotting what she could leverage for spending an evening with dunderheads, and the next moment she was a woman screaming in delight and frantically trying to control her rod and reel.

"I've got one!"

My first reaction was to look up at Sten. He made a scissor gesture, indicating I should cut her line. I smiled. I liked his sentiment but shook my head before turning my attention to Ms. Wonderful.

"Rod tip up. Keep turning the handle." The fish was taking a long run. Line was peeling out of the spool and the drag was properly set. "Just keep turning the handle. If the fish stops and makes a run back at us, reel like crazy until the line is tight again."

"But it's taking all the line! Can't you stop it?"

"That's the idea of playing the fish—you let it take a run then you reel in the line."

"How much line do you have on this rod?"

"Enough."

We played the fish until it swam wearily behind the boat, a little too deep to net. Five feet below the surface in clear water it looked like a silent, translucent ghost entirely unperturbed by the frantic efforts of the woman wearing the toreador hat and sunglasses.

"Get it!" she kept saying. "For God's sake, get it!"

I described how to pump her rod to raise the fish to the waiting net. With some difficulty she coordinated reeling as she dropped her rod tip, then holding the reel handle as she pulled up. To some people it's like trying to rub their stomach and pat their head at the same time. In the end, she managed to bring her salmon close enough to the surface for me to net it.

"Ugh. Why do they have to smell so bad?" was her first comment.

"It certainly isn't their cosmetics," I said under my breath. "This is a chinook—they have a noticeable fish odour of their own. Strong, isn't it?"

She backed up to the bulkhead and leaned her rod against it. Prickles of sweat had formed on her upper lip and more sweat was dripping from her hairline. She pulled a handkerchief from her pocket and lifted it to wipe the perspiration. The motion knocked her stylish sunglasses off her face and into the water.

The landing net still contained her salmon so it could not be used to retrieve the sunglasses. I picked up the gaff but its handle was too short. The glasses started to sink.

"Get them, goddamn you, get them!" she screamed.

"Too late. They're gone." I had seen any number of things go overboard, and I was not about to take the plunge into deep, frigid waters just for a pair of sunglasses, however expensive.

She stormed up to me in a fury. *She's lost it*, I thought.

"You stupid piece of shit! Can't you do anything?" She was so angry that her hands were balled into fists and I thought she was going to spit at me or hit me. She certainly looked like someone about to spit.

I dropped the gaff on the deck and prepared to react. "Cool down, please. You don't want to get hurt over a pair of sunglasses." My voice was sharp, and I was sure she was about to do something stupid. I circled to my right, my hands up in a defensive stance.

"Get those goddamn glasses." Her tone was blistering but I could see she had recognized her situation. She had correctly read me, and she knew if she spat or struck me I would hit her back. Again I saw what a coward she was; she would always back down if someone called her bluff. I imagined that she had struck her husband many times and that he had always accepted her behaviour simply because she was a woman.

At this point he stepped in with a blanket of meaningless words and an arm around her. Pushing him away, she strung together a diatribe of blunt expletives, some of which were new to me. When I looked up at Sten, I saw that the Cardinal was beside him and he was grinning from ear to ear. Looking like a bobble-head, he mouthed her words back at me—*you piece of shit!*—then slammed his right fist into his left palm and pointed at our diva. Once again I smiled and nodded.

The weather had been superb, the tides cooperative and the fishing superb—but the people had been awful. It was time to head in before someone was hurt.

* * *

When I remember items that have gone overboard, I invariably recall the elderly English couple who came out with me on a sunny afternoon. The weather was much like that of the day we had taken out our diva. They were a charming older couple whose dream it had been to visit their daughter in Victoria and fish for a salmon in Canada.

I've often told people that every salmon carries a passport, allowing them to breach all international borders. After all, salmon do not come with a national flag tattooed on their gill flap; they are citizens of the world. It is only the national fisheries, with their financial interests, that try to hand out citizenship cards to the smolt in the headwaters where they hatch.

Yvonne and Jeffrey reminded me of river stones. They were solid and weighty but smoothed by time. Even with their worldly ease, they quivered with giddiness and excitement when I took them into the inlet and gave them each a rod. Shaking like children about to go on their first merry-go-round, they chattered together, egged each other on and threatened to catch the largest salmon Canada had ever seen. Their good-natured banter and enthusiasm made the day memorable and just about perfect.

We had to wait over an hour for our first strike. The salmon had a light touch and was on for only a moment or two, just long enough to bow the rod before throwing the lure. Jeffrey had been somewhat slow when he struck, so I suggested he be more on edge and strike with vigour at anything that remotely felt like a fish. The other guests on board had had similar strikes so I knew the old fellow had reacted well but his timing was a little off.

Less than five minutes later I was standing close to him, chatting with Yvonne, when he snapped up his rod. He did it with such force that his false teeth shot out of his mouth. In disbelief we watched them dance into the depths of the inlet, smiling as they went. Was this happy couple upset? No, they broke into peals of laughter. She immediately accused him of unfair tactics by chumming with his teeth. They were in such fits of hysterics that we were fortunate to land his sleek, sixteen-pound salmon after a serious struggle. When it was finally on deck, they were both so thrilled that they threw their arms around me in a group hug. If ever there was sheer pleasure and joy over fishing, it came from these two octogenarians. When things calmed down a little, Jeffrey shook my hand for the tenth time. He smiled a toothless grin and said he thought he'd made a fair trade with the ocean— his dentures for a sixteen-pound salmon.

"Besides," he added, "those were my old teeth. The new ones are safely at our daughter's house in Victoria."

Lovely weather, cooperative tides, superb fishing and people whose *joie de vivre* was so abundant that nothing could prevent them from having a good time. The perfect combination for a perfect day—and a new home for some tiny crustacean at the bottom of the ocean.

chapter 12

Davy Jones's Locker

Some ideas come to me in a scattered manner. This one came to me out of sheer frustration and in an effort to silence the unending questioning by one of our guests. We were out on a morning charter, we had a few nice salmon on ice, the weather was acceptable and the people were mostly charming. Early on, one of the guests, Joseph, inexplicably glued himself to me and proceeded to question me on all manner of subjects. The questions were random and my answers seemed irrelevant to him. It was as though he was thinking up another question while I was answering his last question.

At one point Joseph asked me what we did with the boat in the off-season. His questioning had been insistent for over half an hour, and I could see it might last for the remainder of the charter if I didn't do something to put an end to it. Without appearing to give it a thought, I quipped, "We do burials at sea. You know—ashes overboard."

That seemed to suck the oxygen out of him. From the corner of my eye I saw Sten spin around and look at me with amusement. He shook his finger in mock admonishment. He had a huge grin on his face; he knew that once I got going I would be selling burial plots in the ocean. In truth the idea was not new to me. Several months earlier, I had made a list of alternate ways to use the boat during the quiet season. Burials at sea was one of the ideas I had written down, researched and rejected—it was probably the reason it popped into my mind just then. In any event Joseph's eyes bulged. I knew I had struck pay dirt.

"Burials at sea?" he repeated in horror, almost in disgust.

"It's a growth industry," I said, trying to sound slick. "I want to be ahead of the curve and secure my market share." I struggled to keep a straight face.

He struck me as one of those MBA types who would buy and sell anything as long as a profit was on hand. The character of Harry Lime from *The Third Man* came to mind; Harry was a man who would dilute penicillin simply to improve his bottom line. As the idea developed in my head, I wondered if I could hold his attention by wafting a delicious margin of profit under his nose. I call salacious profits "MBA Bacon."

The look on Joseph's face was enough to egg me on. He had the sly, secretive expression of a politician incubating a manoeuvre. I watched him pull himself together and digest the idea, weighing the possibilities. I could almost hear his inner dialogue. *There must be a lot of deaths each month on the southern tip of the Island. After all, it's a retirement community. The average funeral expense is around $10,000 a pop. Forty percent profit per body. Hmm, he might be onto something.*

Out loud he said, "How would that work?"

Ah, I thought, *the open-ended question. He wants me to step in and elaborate.* I smiled—artlessly, I hoped—and put my hand on his shoulder. "Does this interest you?"

"It could. How does it work?"

Here we go, I thought, *bodies at a profit.* He had already objectified it. Now it was just a process to him, another means of turning a profit. Why not?—someone has to do it, would be his argument.

"There's not a lot to it," I said. "It's just a question of a little promotion to secure your client base. All your customers will be people holding a jar of ashes they wish to spread in the ocean. There are no actual bodies involved."

This reminded me of the urn that held the ashes of my father. He had loved so many places in the world, and I was uncertain about where to scatter them. It seemed ironic to me that I was pitching this idea to one of our guests, even if it was in jest.

"So where is the money?" he asked.

"In the add-ons," I blurted.

"What do you mean?"

I had to think; I had not really explored the idea that far. "Well, there are all kinds of extras. Do they want clergy involved, do they want it catered, is champagne involved, do they want taped music or live musicians, do they want a floral wreath, clowns, balloons? The list is unending, and you take a commission on every single add-on. There's also the cost of booking the boat and an extra charge if they want extra personnel."

I was making it up as I went along. I could see Joseph was still unconvinced. I hoped he would take this idea and go off to another part of the boat. Instead he turned back to me.

"How would you get your bookings?"

It was clear he was shaping a plan.

"What's your idea?"

"To really develop the business to its full potential, you would need an agent."

I could see where he was going. He was a 10-percenter; he wanted to slide his hand into the middle of the transaction and come away with his 10 percent.

"How would that work?" I asked innocently.

"The agent would bird-dog clients for you by contacting the funeral homes and establishing a referral agreement with them."

"Explain how that would work and how much it would cost."

"The agent brings you the client in return for a fee."

"What would the fee be?"

"Thirty percent of gross."

"Have I got this right? I provide the business idea, the boat, the crew, the amenities and all the services while the agent gets 30 percent of gross for these bookings?"

I happened to look up at Sten and saw that he had retrieved the Cardinal from its storage. One summer, when Sten was in his early teens, he had been involved in a theatrical group that played local venues. An agent who made the bookings was the only person to make money in the endeavour. Sten did not hold agents in high regard.

"I'll have expenses to cover," Joseph said.

"Are we talking about your telephone line, which you already have?"

"There will be my time."

"Ah, your valuable time! How much does that cost per hour?"

"Forty dollars an hour."

Remember, this was in the late 1980s when forty dollars an hour was more than a handsome rate. Hourly rates in those days could range from around three dollars an hour to twelve for people with developed skills. I was mystified by this fellow's 30 percent. As yet I had not unveiled to him the research I had done. It was time to do that.

"When I initially scribbled down this idea," I began, "I made four telephone calls to funeral parlours. Each one of the directors was willing to develop the idea of referring customers to me provided I could demonstrate my service would be on par with theirs. The total amount of time involved was less than one hour.

The follow-up would probably take another hour, and to clinch the deal I would take them all out on a one-hour charter just to show the quality of our service. That would put me in business with them for less than three hundred dollars. From then on it would simply be a question of fielding their referrals. Their commission would be twenty dollars per booked referral. Well under 10 percent."

There was a long silence as Joseph examined me.

"Well, you got me there," he finally said. Without another word, he turned and made his way back to his group. He didn't broach the subject again and he didn't ask me a single question more. Sten was having a grin-athon at the helm and gave me thumbs-up. It's always nice to be appreciated.

Before the group disembarked, the host took me aside to settle our account. After payment had been made, he shook my hand and asked me how I had silenced his friend. In brief I told him the story. He pitched over, laughing, before telling me it was the first time he had seen Joseph silent. When he finally settled down, he pulled a twenty-dollar bill out of his wallet and tried to press it on me.

"Give it to Sten," I said. "He earned it for not banging your friend on the head with the Cardinal."

Sten got the twenty and our host went home with a story to repeat.

"Burials at sea," he kept mumbling as he disembarked.

* * *

On the same subject but in a slightly different vein, we were booked by two brothers who said they wanted the boat to themselves so they could fish quietly together. It was to be an evening charter, and they even designated where they wanted to fish. I wasn't convinced of their choice but thought I would be able to talk them into fishing elsewhere once they were on board.

They arrived in good time and introduced themselves as Bruce and Alphonso. They were in their mid-thirties. Bruce was the eldest; he was also the tallest and wore a moustache and venerable fishing clothes. Alphonso was shorter and balding and was the humorist of the two. He was dressed for a stroll down the Champs Élysées. He was so pressed and starched I wondered whether he would want to touch a fish. There was friendly repartee between them, enough to tell me they liked each other. I relaxed; I could tell this was going to be another nice charter.

The fishing spot they selected was called the Stone House. Down Saanich Inlet, near the shoreline, was a crumbling house built of stone—someone's unfinished dream. A hundred yards directly off this structure was a good fishing spot that oddly had not produced a single fish that season, but that was where they wanted to fish. If we intended to catch a salmon, I thought it prudent to try to change their minds.

The inlet is so beautiful that we usually cruised slowly, taking in the diving birds and bald eagles and watching the shadows change along the shore. Once or twice a year, a grey whale would find its way into the inlet. For reasons better known to whales, one particular fellow would attach himself to our boat and become our shadow, making fishing impossible. On one of these charters, as we were followed by this whale, one of our guests was seen waving at it and shouting, "Shush, shush. Go away, nasty whale." I love optimists with delusions of grandeur.

Bruce and Alphonso stationed themselves at the transom with a giant backpack of treats on the deck between them. During the charter they produced a wide variety of goodies ranging from lengths of licorice to tins of sardines in tomato sauce to a huge assortment of aromatic cheeses with crackers. Most of this was washed down with half bottles of red wine, which they drank from gorgeous, crystal glasses produced from their backpack.

They were an interesting, complex mixture of ribald humour tempered with hard-edged politics. They had both worked extensively in the United States, Brazil and Western Europe. Partners in a high-tech company they'd founded shortly after leaving university, they had convinced their father to postpone his retirement to help them with the nuts and bolts of the business end of their enterprise. To their surprise, the company had grown at an exponential rate, and it was only with the help of their father that they had managed to keep pace with their growth. Most of the past eight years had been spent abroad, establishing contacts and growing their enterprise. They explained that in the past six months they had hired outside talent to replace their father. The idea was to take the business to a new level. While this was happening, they could concentrate on their technical creativity and free themselves from the daily grind of management. Their time working abroad had shifted their view of the world. They were pleased to be back in Canada, but they also realized they no longer viewed the world through a narrow Canadian aperture.

While they were telling me their story and eating unending ropes of licorice, we cruised down the inlet to the Stone House. The bald eagle was sitting on its perch in the tree above us. I pointed it out to them, explaining how we could attract it with a cod. As soon as we came to a halt in front of the Stone House, they dropped their lures to the bottom and started to jig for a cod.

Bruce was quick to throw out a challenge. "The first one to catch a cod gets all the black licorice. The loser has to eat all the red ropes."

I knew we were in an unlikely spot to catch a cod, but I said nothing. Sometimes it was necessary to allow the guests to realize my local knowledge was of some use. In this case I thought it might take as little as a quarter of an hour. Sure enough, it wasn't long before they seemed ready to give up, at which point I suggested they pull in their lines while we moved a couple of hundred yards to an area with a rocky bottom. Within a few minutes we had a cod in the boat. It was about half a pound, the ideal size for an eagle.

Sometimes the performers refuse to perform. The bald eagle paid no attention to my whistles. It sat on its perch, completely uninterested in the cod I was waving over my head. Bruce and Alphonso looked at me skeptically as though questioning my story about throwing a cod. I suggested we put it on ice and try again in a few hours. With the eagle in a funk, I hoped the salmon would be more cooperative.

Both Bruce and Alphonso gave me separate versions of their business lives. At first, neither spoke of their lives before entering university. If they had experienced any of the usual childhood or adolescent trials, they didn't mention them. It was as though they had appeared fully formed in university. The only hint I had about their past was the fact they had inveigled their father to help them in the first phase of their business. Obviously they had a good connection with him, but they said nothing of their mother, grandparents, uncles or aunts. I thought there must be a deeper story, but decided to let them tell it without any probing questions from me.

They both had degrees in computer science. By the time each graduated they had incorporated their business and were researching patents for their inventions. Two young men with prospects, they sailed into the world of business without breaking stride. Their university projects found an immediate home in the competitive business world, which opened doors when they developed future systems. The first few years had been hectic; they had not been prepared for the amount of travel and time spent abroad separately. But they were bright and adaptable and always found ways to develop their projects while maintaining contact with each other.

Above all else they had fun. They loved living in different countries and soon developed a business network with acquaintances in the countries where they worked. The only regret they both expressed was their unilingual education. Alphonso wished he had been taught Portuguese when he was young and Bruce missed not learning German. They could also see that in the future, Mandarin would be a useful language to know.

This story was told to me as we drifted slowly past the Stone House and they devoured the goodies from their bag. I have never seen so much licorice eaten and mused on the effect it had on their systems. Certainly no ill effects manifested themselves while they were on board.

The evening progressed without landing a single salmon. We had two on, but the gods of fishing made sure they were free before we could dip a net into the calm waters and usher them on board. Neither Bruce nor Alphonso was disappointed. They were quite happy to rummage through their backpack and chat about their lives. As the evening unfolded, I realized they were best friends and would probably end their lives living in a house together with each other as company. Their entire focus was on developing their projects and on each other's well-being. It was as though nothing else existed in the world. I mused on the influences that had brought them to this state.

We drifted and we fished. At last, stories unravelled and hints of the brothers' early life began to emerge. Nothing was said directly, only obliquely. It appeared they had come to terms with the divorce of their parents. Their father gained custody and raised them while their mother returned to the land of her birth and started a new family. They lost contact with their mother's side of the family; she became little more than a black and white picture in an old frame sitting on the bedside table. They expressed no sense of loss or rancour at being raised without a mother.

Life goes on in spite of everything, I thought. People like these two brothers never joined support groups. They simply adjusted and got on with life. They certainly gave the impression of being at ease with the world and happy with the life they were making for themselves. I wondered what role their father played in producing these two fine young men.

While it is a tranquil experience to float with the current and chat, it became clear that these two guests would be pleased to have a fish in the boat. I had them pull in their lines while we moved the boat closer to shore. We would make one more drift close to shore, I told them. The drift was going to take us past the Stone House, and they should be prepared to raise their lines if they touched bottom. While they were fishing, I went below to prepare some soup and buns for them and Sten. Sten is one of those fellows who can eat all day without gaining a pound. He is constantly hungry with an appetite for anything other than greasy food, except for french fries. French fries are his nemesis. If you had a packet of french fries with ketchup and a sprinkling of malt vinegar, I believe you could lead Sten into the jaws of death. On this occasion he would have to be content with some homemade soup and fresh wheat buns.

As I was fiddling with the stove and pulling out spoons and soup mugs, I heard some activity on the stern deck. At the wheel, Sten looked down at me and gave a dramatic shrug of his shoulders. I gave him a questioning look, but he simply repeated the gesture. Obviously it was nothing urgent, so I continued with the preparation for the meal. When the soup and buns were hot, I carried a tray with the food to our guests at the stern.

As I put the plates on the transom, I looked at the two men to announce dinner was ready. They stood on the other side of the boat staring back at me. Their rods were neatly in their holders. They looked like two schoolboys caught smoking behind the gym. I could imagine that was exactly how they had looked when they were fifteen or sixteen.

I almost said, "What have you two boys been up to?" Instead I looked around for a clue.

We were drifting slowly past the Stone House. The ocean, at the stern of the boat, was covered with an unusual white skim that I could not identify. I looked up at Sten. He gave me the same dramatic shrug. The only thing that came to mind was pollen, but it was the wrong time of year. The two men looked terribly self-conscious. In fact, they looked guilty.

"Did you throw something overboard?" I asked.

They squirmed. I could not help smiling. They had completely reverted back to their teens.

"We didn't know how you would feel, so we just went ahead and did it." The elder brother Bruce was doing the talking; Alphonso would not meet my gaze.

"What did you throw overboard?"

Again Bruce spoke. "It was our father's ashes."

The scenario fell into place. Earlier they'd told me their father had been replaced in their company, but they had not explained why. I had assumed it was because he wanted to retire.

I had one more question. "Why the Stone House?"

"When we were just kids," Bruce said, "this is where Dad used to take us when we went fishing. He said it was a hot spot. I think we always came home with a salmon."

Alphonso was working hard not to cry. He stared at the ashes floating at the stern of the boat as they gradually dissolved into the water.

Bruce put an arm over his brother's shoulders. "Dad always said this was the most perfect place in the world. When something goes right for Alphonso and me, we always say 'Stone House' for good luck."

I watched these two young men, enveloped in the memory of their father, with his ashes dissolving into the ocean behind us.

"Would you like me to say some words?"

"It's okay. We've said them."

"Is there anything I can do?"

"No, we're all right."

"Do you want to go in?"

The brothers looked at each other. With his arm still around Alphonso, Bruce said, "How about we catch and land a nice one."

"Let's do it." This time it was Sten joining in the conversation.

"What was your dad's name?" I asked.

"He was called John Henry, but his real name was Eustace Jean. Don't laugh. We never heard him called anything but John Henry or JH. The name suited him—he was a big, strong, clever man, right until the end. A heart attack followed by a massive stroke took him. It was sudden and a surprise to all of us. Thank goodness we were close when it happened." There was a quiet sense of grief in Bruce's tone; the loss was still fresh. "We sure miss him. He was always there for us. It's hard to realize he's gone forever."

They were still gazing at the dissipating film of ashes on the water. I could not think of much to say that would help this moment. I walked over to them, put my arms around both of them and said, "My dad's gone too. I still miss him. Dads are so special."

The brothers sighed heavily.

Bruce broke the sombre mood. "So let's catch a fat salmon off the Stone House."

"A fat salmon," I echoed. I had not heard anyone say that for a long time.

Sten fired up the engine and put us in slow forward. The stern of our boat eased away from the remaining dust on the surface. Bruce and Alphonso watched our slow movement away from the remnants of their father's ashes.

"It's exactly where he wanted to be, isn't it?" Alphonso said to his brother.

"It's perfect. The time of day is perfect, the weather is perfect— it's all perfect."

Sten moved us slowly to the hot spot in front of the Stone House. He took a look at the paper sounder. "Bait at eighty feet," he called out in surprise.

Everyone picked up a rod and started to count pulls.

"Salmon showing under the bait," Sten said.

Ultimately, after serious difficulties, we caught a twenty-five pounder. It was the only salmon we caught in that spot all year. After our catch, the eagle that had been ignoring us for hours finally cooperated, swooping down from its perch to snatch our cod from the surface of the water. Of many nearly perfect days in the history of Magna Charters, this one was possibly the most perfect of all.

* * *

A charter boat seems to attract all kinds of strange attention. It is not unusual to have tourists approach the skipper of a charter boat and ask him for fishing tips. I saw no harm in giving out information, although I never told these visitors the precise locations where they should fish. I might tell them to fish in a kelp bed, but I would omit telling them about the deep spot where heavy salmon sometimes rested when the current was at full flood.

One afternoon, I was brought to the aft deck by some serious banging on the side of my boat. It was a pounding with a sense of urgency. The source of this noise was a wiry, ferret-like woman in her mid-sixties. It was a hot summer day, yet she wore a heavy plaid overcoat that hung well below her knees. On either side of her large, beaked nose were two darting eyes that couldn't seem to settle on a single object. Even as she spoke to me, her eyes darted around, never once making contact with mine. Under her coat I could see she was quivering. Her hands fluttered around, touching her face then dusting off her coat. She was in constant motion. I hoped she wanted only information and not to book a charter.

"How much do you charge?" There was no greeting, no preamble.

"How long would you want to be out?"

"We only want to go out for an hour."

"We don't go out an hour at a time. We have a flat rate that covers four hours."

"I'll give you twenty bucks to take us out for an hour—cash!"

Her tone was insistent, almost belligerent. As she spoke she became even more agitated. The corners of her mouth turned down and her hands flew about her face and tugged at the buttons on her coat. Behind her, four or five people were slowly making their way down the dock to my slip.

"Are those your friends?" I asked.

She barely looked over her shoulder. "Yeah, they are."

"We only go out for a minimum of four hours, and we're booked for this afternoon."

As if she hadn't heard me, she said, "Okay, I'll give you twenty-five bucks to take us out for an hour." She was almost crawling onto the boat. I stepped in front of her and blocked her way.

"We're already booked, I said, "and I do not go out for a single hour."

By then her group was standing on the dock beside the boat. They looked very much like her. It was as though they had all just rolled out of a common bed and come straight to the marina. There was a dank smell about them, an unwashed quality. I regretted Sten's absence. I could see this could escalate into a nasty situation, so I decided my best solution was to offer them another option. But what?

Before I could say a word, a member of the group stepped beside the woman, fixed his eyes on mine and asked in an angry tone, "What's wrong? Isn't our money good enough for you?"

Ah, a chip on his shoulder, I thought. He saw a big, luxurious boat with a clean-cut skipper blocking his way so he registered this as a threat. I knew I had to come up with an option or the chip on their collective shoulders would become a plank.

"What do you want to do once we're away from the dock?" I asked.

"Throw my dad's ashes overboard. It'll only take a minute."

The blunt frankness of the ferret woman surprised me. I smiled—I knew just what to do. "Do you see that boat moored astern of me?" I pointed at the gorgeous thirty-four-foot double ender. "I'll bet the owner will be more than pleased to take you out for twenty-five dollars."

The focus of the group shifted from me to the double ender.

"He's not on board right now," I said, "but he usually comes down to check on his boat around six every evening. I'll be out on the water with my party, but I'm sure he'll be willing to take you for an hour."

"You sure? You're not just saying that to get rid of us?" the ferret woman asked.

She was right, of course. I was steering her away from my boat, but I also knew the owner of the double ender would take anyone out for any sum of money. He was a conscientious drinker, and during the summer months I frequently had to throw a blanket over him in the evening and turn off the lights on his boat.

He was an affable man who happened to drink too much, and like many heavy drinkers, he was often in tears over his condition.

Later that afternoon my group arrived, and we set off under ideal conditions to catch some salmon and listen to stories. There was not a puff of wind when we left. The air was heavy, but the fishing was steady.

We were moored half an hour before dark because a stiff wind had come up. By the time we were at the dock, the fish were bagged and the boat was washed down. The guests stayed on board to have a sundowner and extend a good day on the water.

I was sitting on the transom, listening to the chatter and relaxing. Out of the corner of my eye I saw the green and white double ender bearing down on us. It was heading straight for us. On its present course it would strike us amidships. I shouted for everyone to get off the boat and stood on the port rail, yelling and waving my arms. The double ender changed course just in time to avoid a collision. But heading into its slip behind us, its forward progress was far too great and another collision loomed.

I vaulted over my rails onto the dock and called to my guests to give me a hand pushing the double ender away from the dock and along its slip. I hoped like hell the skipper would have the good sense to throw his engine into reverse.

On cue, just seconds before his bow ploughed into the dock, the engine was slammed into reverse, slowing the boat and allowing us to push the hull alongside the dock without any harm done either to the dock or to us. I secured the boat and started back to the *Kalua* when I heard a familiar voice.

"He kept us out for two and a half hours for twenty-five bucks." The voice of the ferret woman was slurred and held the sharp edge of an insult.

I walked back to her. I could see into the stateroom. Clothes and empty bottles were strewn on the floor. The vessel reeked of alcohol. I mentally patted myself on the back for having nothing to do with these people.

Her entire group came to the stern deck where she was standing. The smell of unwashed bodies and alcohol was stifling. As a group they looked in worse condition than when I had first seen them.

"Did you have a good time?" I asked.

In the fading pre-sunset light I could see their drunken smiles. They all grinned lopsidedly and clung to one another, rocking with the movement of the boat. Strangely, their faces and hair looked as though they had been powdered, and a dark grit filled the cracks between their teeth. A proud, dishevelled group stood on the deck, leering at me.

Ah, ordinary people. Deliver us from ordinary people.

Suddenly I realized what had happened. Their drunken skipper had thrown the ashes of the ferret woman's father into the wind. All the ashes had blown back directly into their faces, filling the cracks between their teeth and powdering their faces and hair with coarse grey ash.

All that for just twenty-five dollars. What a deal!

chapter 13
A Connecting Rod

When my father was in his early eighties he had a serious heart attack. On his return home from the hospital, with monitoring devices and nitrate patches, he set about his rehabilitation with the calm tenacity he had shown all his life. Within a few months he was walking across The Links at Victoria Golf Course to one of his favourite shoreline fishing spots, a place we called Flat Rock. I told him that once we could make the walk to Flat Rock together without stopping to rest, I would take him out on the boat. Within a short time he was fit enough to take me up on my offer.

I delayed the fishing expedition to coincide with a visit from my brother, Alan, who was flying in from North Carolina to see Dad. When he arrived, the weather conditions were unreliable so we waited nearly a week before going out. My mother was not included since she was prone to serious bouts of motion sickness. The crew would consist of just my father, my brother and me. On the day of our trip high tide was around four in the afternoon, so by three we were on the boat and ready to cast off.

My fishing contacts suggested the best starting place was Willis Point. I assembled three drift-fishing rods. One was a light, whippy spinning rod my father had commissioned from a tackle shop in Paris, France, that Alan and I used as boys. It was of man-made material with a perfect taper and all the original finish. It even had the original cork handle and ferrules. I selected this rod for my father and paired it with a light, open-faced reel. With an overcast sky and no wind, conditions were superb for fishing.

In hindsight, considering my father's health, I am amazed at how lighthearted we were. The three of us had spent innumerable hours fishing together and although we had gone our separate ways, the memories of fishing the rivers of Europe and the UK gave us common ground. Alan told some of his stories about fishing in Ireland with Dad, stories I had never heard. It was fresh material that gave me more insight into my brother and his relationship with our father. Like mine, it was a complex but loving relationship. Drifting through the quiet waters of the inlet, we reminisced over common events and poked good-natured fun at each other. While the paper sounder showed baitfish under us, no one had a touch. I changed lures and altered our fishing depth. Nothing helped, so after an hour we pulled in our lines and sat around the dinette table, where we had a hot drink and ate the picnic lunch Mum had kindly prepared for us. The three of us shared a meal and a comfortable camaraderie talking about things in our lives that gave us pleasure. We had reached a point where we were no longer a father and two brothers. We were three men with our own lives, sharing a lunch and talking about things that connected us.

After our snack I looked over the side of the boat and saw semi-translucent squid pulsing in the water around us. On previous occasions when squid were present, I had done well off a nearby point that was just a few minutes from our present location, so I fired up the engine and moved the boat. Within ten minutes Dad had a fish on. Alan and I put down our rods and watched the old master at work. The rod and the fish were well-suited, and in spite of their ages, both the rod and the fisherman had plenty of spring. It was like watching the easy grace of a perfectly matched couple on a ballroom floor. They worked in effortless harmony, moving to and from each other. There was no stress until the last moments when the fisherman steered his partner into the abyss of the net and I swung it on board.

Just before I sent the fish home with a blow from the Priest, I heard my father moan. Puzzled, I looked up at him. There was genuine sorrow on his face as he stared at the salmon, with the treble hooks deep in its throat and entangled in its gills. It would never survive in the ocean if it was released. I dispatched it with a bang on the head and my parting blessing, "Go home, now," then held it up for Dad to see. He had already turned and was inspecting the rod that had helped him land his salmon.

"This is a good little rod. It's got a great action."

My mind slipped back forty years. We were on Easter holiday from our dreaded school in Switzerland. We'd been home for a few days and felt a surprise was in the air, but no matter how we tried to discover it, no one would tell us what it was going to be. Even our mother, who could never keep a secret, refused to say anything. Then one afternoon Dad's keys rattled in the front door. I ran to greet him. I was certain he would have two freshly baked baguettes with the crusty end of one of them missing. The baguettes seldom made it home intact.

On this occasion, however, Dad had what was obviously a fishing rod in its cloth carrying case tucked under one arm. He was juggling the keys to the apartment and the bread with his free arm.

"What's that?" we asked.

"I'll show you in a minute." He took the baguettes to the kitchen and returned to the living room, where he put the rod on the huge square centre table. With a couple of quick pulls, the tabs of the cloth case were undone and the two parts of the rod slipped out. He lined up the ferrules and pushed the two ends together.

"It's beautiful," I said, my voice hushed with wonder.

Today, gazing at my father's back and remembering this long-ago incident, my words echoed from the past. "It's a beautiful little rod."

"Yes, it is—but a bit beaten-up."

"It's seen a lot of life and caught a lot of fish."

He turned to me with that faint, amused smile I knew so well. "So have I."

Several months after this little rod came to our Paris apartment, I was fishing with it in one of the many fast-running rivers my father had discovered in France. While I had fished countless hours for a trout, I had never caught one. I had a sense of despair; I was truly starting to think that I was jinxed and would never catch a trout. Standing on a low bridge, with the clear water of the rushing river cascading over smooth stones beneath my feet, I allowed my line to be carried downstream. I was simply going through the motions of fishing, by now not expecting anything to happen. I slowly turned the handle of my reel, which clicked the bail into the retrieve position. As I did so, I felt the Mepps spinner twirling at the end of my line with a slight vibration and an occasional tug. I was so despondent that I paid little attention but continued to reel in the line. As I reeled I looked downstream. There, the largest, most beautiful trout I had ever seen in my life was swimming up toward the bridge. With almost superhuman energy, I immediately started to reel in my line. I wanted to retrieve my lure and cast it at the trout before it passed under the bridge and out of sight. As I reeled, I kept track of the trout.

Two things happened at the same time. First the trout flicked its head to one side, then I felt a strong tug at the end of my line. I was in complete disbelief. I knew by the tug and the bow of the rod that the trout was on. It had taken my lure farther down-stream and was swimming upstream with it. From that moment to the moment I beached the trout, I made every error imagin-able. Fortunately the trout went upstream and under the bridge only once; the rest of the time it chose to make its stand right in front of me so I could see it darting from one rock to another in the clear rippling water. It was truly a push-me-pull-me situa-tion. On one hand I wanted desperately to land the fish, and on the other I was moved by its battle to live. Our new little trout rod covered my innumerable errors. It cushioned the surges and runs of the fish when my drag was too tight and kept pressure on the fish as it battled to stay in the water. The whole episode did not last ten minutes, yet the memory has remained fresh in my mind all these years.

Now, here I was on my boat in Canada, with my father's sal-mon on the deck and Dad admiring that same trout rod.

"Do you remember when you brought this rod home?"

He picked it up and tried to read the label on the rod without using his glasses. "No. It feels French."

Alan and I cracked up. "The people at Au Coin de Pêche made it for you in Paris," I said to jog his memory.

"It's a man-made blank, not split cane," he said with some disappointment.

"You had it specially made for Alan and me. You said you wanted something indestructible."

"Hmm. Well, it's not split cane but it has a good action."

I don't know quite why this little scene aboard the *Kalua* gives me so much pleasure. I smile every time I recall it, perhaps be-cause it in turn brings memories of using that rod as a child in France and later, as a young man in Ireland.

At the end of my junior year of college in the United States, I paid my parents an extended visit in London, where they were living at the time. I secured a job at a remand home working with delinquent children. In hindsight, it was the wrong place for me to be. I found the conditions to be something out of a Charles Dickens novel. While I needed the job, my colleagues and the bureaucracy irked me with their narrow view of care. Working with Babbitt-like people whose sole purpose was to retain their jobs bothered me to the point of combustion.

After I'd been working there for nearly four months, my father asked me if I would like to join him for a three-day fishing break in Ireland. I told him I had not saved enough money for such an adventure. In fact, the idea of saving money didn't occur to me in those days. Dad kindly offered to cover my costs. I jumped at the chance to get away from work and told the idiot who was my supervisor some rot about an aunt being ill. I did have an aunt living near Tunbridge Wells, but at the age of seventy-four she could mend her own roof. In truth I did not expect to have a job when I returned.

Off Dad and I went to fish the Blackwater River in County Kerry, southern Ireland. I took the little trout rod while Dad took a small collection of split cane, spinning rods and a few fly rods.

When we reached the banks of the Blackwater, Dad went upstream with his gillie—the local fishing guide. I sat in the long grass along the bank, listening to the river and watching the birds darting over the surface of the fast-moving water. The river was murky and in flood, and I could see little reason to cast a line unless a migrating salmon showed itself. Running parallel to the main river was a five-foot-wide feeder stream with fast-flowing water. The sound of the two bodies of water running side by side was braided into a single noise interrupted only by the occasional splash of a salmon breaching. Each time I heard a salmon breach I prepared to cast. This went on for over an hour, during which time I made only one or two casts, enough to make me realize the gears in my reel were suspect. I had picked the wrong one from our tackle box, which was now upriver with my father and his gillie.

Just then, looking down the feeder stream, I saw the dorsal fin of a salmon working its way up toward me. My first cast was too long so I quickly retrieved the line and cast again, this time a few feet ahead of the migrating fish. Without hesitating, the salmon put on a burst of speed and took the lure. This has always amazed me because Atlantic salmon do not feed when in fresh water. As soon as the salmon realized its mistake, it turned and headed downstream. I threw open my bail and allowed the line to be taken without any resistance. At the junction of the Blackwater, the fish turned and began making its way back up the feeder stream. My reason for letting the line run out was to take all pressure off the fish. Most combative fish will struggle against the pressure from the fisherman. When the pressure is lifted, chances are the fish will return to its original course.

That was exactly what this salmon did. As it swam back upstream, I reeled in the loose line as quickly as I could. The inevitable occurred—the questionable mechanism in the reel seized. The handle froze in mid-turn as the salmon swam toward me. There was nothing else to do except play it by hand—the reel was useless. I clamped the butt of the rod between my knees and retrieved the line using both hands, forming coils of it in the long grass around me. When I was back in touch with the fish I played it delicately. Monofilament line has a way of forming its own Gordian knot. As I sprinted along the bank of the stream to keep up with the fish, dragging coils of monofilament behind me, it inevitably caught in the grass, picked up small branches and eventually snapped.

The line was still running through the ferrules, so I held the rod in my right hand and the broken end of the line in my

left. I could not help chuckling. Instead of letting line stream
out when the fish spurted upstream, I had to run along the bank.
Similarly, when it swam downstream I had to trot back along
the bank to keep up with it. This comedy routine went on for
ten minutes. It was not the elegant fishing style a gillie
would expect from his charge. I was relieved both my father and
his gillie were too far away to see the playing of the fish or the
awkward netting of it. I was singularly pleased when they
returned an hour later without a fish and I was able to show
them my beautiful six-pound grilse, which I had placed in the
tall grass beside me. I did not tell the gillie how it was played; it
was only after dinner that night, with a Drambuie in hand, that
I told my father about the ridiculous comedy that had unfolded
that afternoon. He shook his head, laughing, and complimented
me on my ingenuity.

Now, as I cleaned my father's salmon in the trough at the
stern of the boat, I reminded Dad of this episode in Ireland and
how I had used the rod that had just landed his salmon here in
Canada. He picked up the rod and turned it over in his hand, then
felt its action by bowing the rod on the deck.

"I remember. I dined out on that story many times. I can
remember how pleased you were with yourself. I can still see
you grinning as we admired your catch lying in the grass. You
certainly earned that one."

Even as a man in my late forties, I felt inordinately pleased
to hear a compliment like that from my father.

* * *

Several months later, Dad died from a second heart attack. I
stowed away all his fishing gear along with the whippy little trout
rod that had caught his last salmon. I hadn't the heart to take it

out of storage until several years later when my daughter Anna needed a suitable rod to use on the boat. That whippy wee rod is now in Washington State, where Anna lives. For many years she used it aboard the *Kalua*, giving it a huge workout catching beautiful salmon.

Fathers are prone to hyperbole when speaking of their children. But it's no exaggeration to say that Anna is a natural, vibrating fisherwoman. There is no pretext to her fishing; she does not fish to please her father. She simply loves to fish, and she loves to catch fish. When I'm out with Christine and Anna, it never crosses my mind that they are out on the water only to provide me with company. They both love to be there and they are good at fishing.

When we took guests out on a charter, Anna and I developed a routine that tied into my instructional patter at the start of each charter. I would tell our guests how to handle the gear while Anna demonstrated what I said. She is now a working actress, so you can imagine her panache when she showed how the gear should be used.

During one of these demonstrations we were both standing at the stern of the boat, where I was delivering my lecture while Anna showed how to strip out the line while counting pulls.

At one point she interrupted me. "Dad, I'm sure I have a fish on." Anna was only thirteen at the time but very self-assured.

We were in reasonably shallow water, so my first thought was that she had hooked bottom. When I looked at her line I could see several coils of it on the surface. "It's fairly shallow here. How many pulls did you count?"

"Twenty."

This conversation stirred the guests, who were standing in a semicircle around Anna and me.

"Reel in," I suggested. "See what happens."

No sooner had she turned the handle on the reel four or five cranks than a large salmon burst out of the water astern of us and landed on its side with a dramatic splash.

Line began peeling out of the reel; I loosened the drag a fraction to let the salmon run. The fish sounded, making the spool sing and putting a strain on my little girl's arm. She was standing straight, allowing the line to run out. When I touched the tip of her wee rod, she immediately raised the angle to allow the rod to do its work.

The guests started to participate in the playing of the fish. They cheered Anna on but gave her lots of room to move. At one point I picked her up and carried her to the upper deck to make it easier for her to play the fish. She was on the port side standing at the railing when the salmon turned abruptly, sounded and came steaming back to the boat. It went under us, dragging line against the shoe of the keel.

"Go to the lower deck," I suggested as I took the rod out of her hands. "I'll try to clear the line away from the prop."

Anna nearly jumped to the lower deck. I followed her, holding the rod straight up and well above my head. I went to the port side and tightened the line, then dipped the rod as far as I could into the ocean and walked around the stern, keeping the line away from the propeller. We were lucky the line didn't snag on the prop, and Anna got her rod back with her feisty fish peeling line from the spool. It was a marvellous sight—this strong girl holding onto her doubled-over rod, the line screaming away from her and throwing up a fine spray.

At that point I leaned forward and asked, "Do you want me to take the rod?" It was my standard question to all our guests and was always spoken with what I imagined was a demonic glint in my eye. Few people ever gave up their rod and Anna was no exception. She was not about to let her father play her fish.

"Catch your own fish," she said, loud enough for everyone to hear.

"Come on, let me give you a break," I insisted.

"I don't need a break. Catch your own fish." She was smiling. I loved this banter. I loved it even more when I was dealing with my children. They always knew what was coming and always gave me grief.

The guests had scuttled down to the forward cabin to retrieve their cameras while still cheering on the slight girl with the little rod and the big fish at the end of her line. It was not until Anna brought her fish alongside the boat and I netted it that I realized just how excited everyone was. I looked up at Sten. He held up a count of ten fingers plus eight. I hoped it would go twenty but Sten was right. It was exactly eighteen pounds and had taken nearly thirty-five minutes to land.

Anna's right arm was very sore and her hand was blistered, but she knew there would be little sympathy if she complained, not with an eighteen-pound salmon on the deck. She spent the rest of the charter at the helm, rubbing her overworked right arm but with a grin stretched across her face. Her grin grew even larger when she later showed her salmon to her grandfather. He gave her a squeeze and complimented her on her unblemished, gleaming salmon. Kind words and recognition from Grandpa meant a lot.

* * *

The following day Anna and I were back on the *Kalua* for a late-afternoon charter. The group was made up of what Anna called "manly men." They were a kind, friendly group but definitely on the manly side. Taken with a sense of humour, they were fun to watch as each demonstrated to the other men that he was a real man. They did not go so far as to beat on their chests, but they certainly carried their cans of beer with testosterone-fuelled swagger. With all this display there was no harm and lots of humour. I knew it would be a good charter.

On the way out I told our guests about the salmon Anna had caught the previous day. They were all fathers with children of their own and they understood my excitement and pride. "Let's hope she can do the same today," one of the guests said. In my heart I sincerely wished she would catch another one the same size because it had been so much fun sharing her excitement.

"Everyone will have a chance to catch one in that range. Today we're going to Sheppard Point, where we caught the eighteen pounder yesterday. Anything less than eighteen pounds will be returned to the ocean."

This last remark of mine brought a murmur of dissent from the group. I think they missed my little joke. They immediately wanted to know the legal size for keeping a salmon and how many they could catch and keep. I explained that on board the *Kalua* the chinook had to be around five pounds and the coho in the three- to four-pound range. The bag limit was four of each but I always urged guests to release the fish they were not going to use. The general opinion in this group was that they would not consider releasing any regulation-weight salmon until they had landed—and kept—the first one.

Often the tide does not work to your schedule. According to my estimation, that day it was late in changing. When we arrived at our destination, the tide change was boiling around us. Drift fishing was out of the question, so we brought out the trolling gear and set up the downriggers, hooking up two rods and trolling with our lures around eighty feet. Patches of feed were evident at that depth but they had not concentrated into large shoals. I was not very hopeful.

Then, as if to prove that pessimism seldom prevails, the port-side downrigger bell rang and the line was immediately released. I picked up the rod, reeled in the slack line and handed it off to a short, bearded man who insisted upon being called Ace. A perpetually smiling fellow, he wore an engineer's cap and coveralls. The outfit looked incongruous with his stylish white deck shoes.

Between the strong tide and the trolling gear, the seven-pound salmon put up little resistance. It was good to have a sparkling clean salmon on ice, and the smell of skunk dissipated.

Sten repositioned us over the school of herring that had produced our first salmon, and during the next half an hour we pulled in two more seven to eight pounders. All three fish were stuffed full of herring. They were in beautiful "show" condition, meaning they were free of net marks and seal bites and could be put in a television commercial as the quintessential example of a salmon. They were sleek, gorgeous and flawless.

Pleased with the fish, the men began to relax and enjoy the scenery and one another's company. Stories and family histories started to unfold. The inevitable pictures came out of their wallets and soft, loving stories about their children were shared. During all this talk, I saw Sten give me the "up" sign to reel in the lines and store the downriggers. The tide action was easing and we could now head to our intended fishing location. Anna pitched in and retrieved the line on both rods while I cranked in the fifteen-pound weights on the downriggers. When the trolling gear was stored, Sten took us to our drift-fishing spot while Anna brought out the drift-fishing gear.

This, I thought, *is when the charter really begins.*

On this day Anna was using her wee rod and the same lure that had caught her eighteen pounder the previous day. I hoped the rod still had good juju. Some of the paint was missing and the base had a slight bend to it. She had taken the precaution of retying the knot to the lure and sharpening the hooks. I said nothing but was bursting with pride that she was acting on her own.

"Which is my rod?" Ace asked. He had stepped away from the group of men on the stern deck. I picked up one of the rods Anna had set out and handed it to him.

"This is the hot rod. The lure on it has caught four or five twenty pounders in the past week. If you don't catch one in that range I'll throw you overboard."

He looked at me, a bit startled, then saw the laughter in my eyes and smiled. "That sounds like a vote of confidence. Twenty pounds would suit me fine," he said.

"I hope you catch your twenty pounder, but my money is on Anna. She has a good touch and luck is running with her right now."

Ace looked over at Anna, who was handing out rods to the guests. He nodded his head at her. "She sure has the confidence to catch one."

With the slackening of the tide, the baitfish moved closer to the surface, so we were fishing around forty feet. There was so much bait underneath us the fishermen could feel it bumping into their lines. Since I will fish for almost anything I put on a herring jig and caught a dozen herring to use as bait. A live herring, at the end of a float, is an exciting way to fish. You can see where the herring is swimming, and when a salmon takes your bait the float bobs out of sight.

The float acted as a focus of attention. While everyone was fishing they kept an eye on it. The inevitable questions were asked. They wanted to know if live herring caught more fish than artificial lures or if trolling produced more fish than drift fishing. As the conversation rolled on, I explained why we fished in certain ways and how the choices were made. The short answer is that if the salmon are concentrated by baitfish, drift fishing is the most productive way to fish, but if the fish are scattered then trolling tends to produce more fish. It is a rule of thumb, not a thundering Evangelical Truth.

At one point during this conversation, I interjected that hand grenades were truly the most efficient way to catch salmon. I rattled on but could see the look of consternation on their faces. Finally, Joshua, who was the host of the party, shook his head and squinted his eyes as he asked, "Did you say hand grenades?"

"Yes," I answered, my voice deadpan. "Of course, we use a seven-second fuse. We never use three-second fuses—that would be far too dangerous."

I kept talking but they were clearly still confused. My answer had been so glib they were mulling over the idea and wondering if I might actually be serious.

"Is that legal?" Joshua asked hesitantly.

"Oh no. It's quite illegal but very productive," I answered as lightly as I could. I kept prattling on about fishing techniques but I had lost their attention. They were still working over the idea of using hand grenades to catch salmon.

I saw a flash of recognition from Joshua.

Oh-oh, the jig is up, I thought. *Time to 'fess up that I'm pulling their leg.*

"I thought salmon sank when there's a concussion underwater. It has to do with their air bladder or lack of one or something like that," he said.

I didn't go into the anatomy of a salmon but thought, *the game is still on*. It was time to take it one step further.

"You're absolutely right," I said. "That's why we always carry scuba gear on board. Sten is certified so after we've dropped a hand grenade or two overboard, he slides into the water with a diving basket and collects whatever we need. It's like going to the supermarket. It's very efficient, and it saves a ton on fuel."

The entire group of manly men looked frozen in motion. They half believed me, yet they were still uncertain.

Anna and Sten were struggling to keep a straight face. I didn't know how much longer I could keep up the deception.

Ace gave me a long look. "You're kidding, right?"

"Right!"

"You mean you're kidding about the grenades?"

I'd kept a straight face far too long. Now, I couldn't contain my grin. "You're right, we don't use hand grenades. We use dynamite."

"You're kidding?"

"Right."

I still had him confused and uncertain. "You're kidding, aren't you?"

"Of course I'm kidding."

General laughter rippled through the group. No doubt they were still unsure whether I was going to pitch a couple of sticks of explosive overboard while they were out with me.

"I wouldn't dream of tossing explosives overboard when I'm using live bait."

The group focused again. Ace looked perplexed.

Joshua piped up. "Are you saying that you do or you don't use explosives?" It sounded like his attempt at a firm voice.

Meanwhile, Anna had migrated to the helm, where she and Sten were listening to my antics.

"We absolutely do not use explosives," I said solemnly. "Salmon sink too quickly."

A palpable sigh of relief could be felt through the group. Up at the helm, Sten and Anna gave each other a high-five. Anna came down to the stern deck and flashed a grin at Joshua. "Dad gotcha, didn't he?"

"He had me going there for a minute. It's hard to be sure what to expect from your dad."

Anna smiled. "I taught him everything he knows."

The group laughed. My darling daughter had captured their attention in a way I could never have done.

"Then teach me how to catch a twenty pounder," Ace said.

With that, Anna strode over to where he had his line in the water and asked him how many pulls he had let out.

"I lost count," he said.

"Reel in and count twenty pulls." She watched him reel in his line and as he counted out the twenty pulls. When that was done she took the rod out of his hand and demonstrated how to get the right action with the lure. "Most of the time, they take it when it's tumbling down. So be ready to strike when you start to bring it back up. Strike and keep your rod tip up."

In that moment, I was blind to anything but a father's joy and pride. What happened next was a fisherman's dream. Ace turned his attention to his rod and precisely followed Anna's instructions. He raised his rod tip, dragged the lure up two feet then dropped it suddenly, allowing the lure to flutter down in imitation of a wounded herring.

When he went to raise it again, he felt the heavy weight of a salmon and his rod bowed over. "Fish on!" he shouted and inexplicably threw his cap on the deck.

Anna reached over and checked the tension on his reel. It was perfectly set. She pulled her hand away as the salmon took off, screaming out line and heading out to sea. There was no doubt about the authority of this fish. This was the one we were hoping for. I had a moment of regret—I wanted Anna to be the person who hooked it.

Even as Ace's fish was taking its first run, his friends began to rib him. I stood just behind him and whispered instructions as they were needed. He was confident about how to play the fish; he only needed to relax a bit and allow the salmon to tire itself out. It was a powerful fish with the authority that years of survival had given it. At this stage we were just bystanders, waiting for the salmon to exhaust itself in its battle for life.

Ace was neither tall nor big, as I've noted. His coveralls and railway cap, which was now lying on the deck, emphasized his short stature and gave him the appearance of a preteen boy. Standing by the transom with his back to his friends and a rod doubled over, he truly looked like a little boy playing a big fish. As might be expected, his size and appearance became the butt of his friends' jokes.

"I've got twenty bucks that says the fish is bigger than you," said one of his friends.

"The next run it takes will lift you over the rail," said another.

Ace paid little attention to these remarks. He was totally absorbed in landing his fish.

I kept up a quiet commentary behind him, my voice at a low pitch so only he could hear me. "That's right—keep your line tight and your tip up. Don't give him any slack. We don't know how well he's hooked."

Most of what I said was to reassure him. He was terribly anxious and kept repeating that he simply must land this fish. It dawned on me that more was at stake than catching a salmon. Almost nothing is ever what it seems to be. I had no idea what was at work in this fisherman's mind, but I could tell it was causing him so much anxiety that he wasn't truly enjoying the excitement of the moment.

"Does it feel like a big fish?" I asked, trying to refocus him.

"It's heavy and strong," he answered, almost to himself.

"What makes you say that?"

The salmon turned and scribed a semicircle course at the stern of the boat. The fish was about eighty feet out and forty feet down. Ace was holding his rod straight up, putting maximum pressure on the fish.

"You've done this before?" I asked.

"Yeah, but I never landed one. I never caught a salmon this size. This is one monster fish." He was panting as he spoke and quivering from the adrenalin.

The other guests were standing away from him, giving him lots of room, but they continued to tease him with suggestions. Putting my index finger to my lips, I indicated they should withhold their comments for the time being. I held my arms out as wide as I could in an effort to emphasize the size of the salmon. As a group they smiled and gave me thumbs-up.

Anna was at the helm with Sten; both of them were beside themselves with excitement. I held up five fingers then a zero. I was guessing, since the largest salmon we had landed was forty-five pounds and I knew this one had to be heavier. The guests watched this exchange between Sten and me, and it appeared to raise their level of excitement. Cans of beer were lifted in a silent toast.

Meanwhile, Ace moved to the centre of the transom. His salmon was sounding as it came closer to the boat, and he brought in line as fast as he could. At the same time, he kept glancing at me for approval.

"You're doing fine," I said. "Just stay in contact with it."

He was a good fisherman with good instincts; he kept his line tight and his rod tip up. The margin between a good fisherman and a novice is small. A good fisherman can relax and still stay in contact with the fish. Ace was starting to relax. There was almost a smile on his face when the salmon sounded again, spinning line out of his spool and spraying his hand with salt water.

"We need four or five of those runs to tire him out," I said.

"Damn, he's strong!" Ace said. "I can't believe how strong he is."

As fast as the line was dragged out, Ace had to reel it back in when the salmon headed for the surface. This to and fro battle continued for over three-quarters of an hour. We never had to chase it. A couple of times Sten jogged the boat around a little bit so the fish was always astern of us. Some of the other guests went to the bow and put down a line in hopes of catching a twin to the one we had on. They didn't get in the way so there was never a chance of tangling lines.

I knew the fish was exhausted when it finally swam directly astern of us about ten feet under water. Its runs were brief and the line was easily retrieved. I thought it might be only a few minutes before we got our chance to net it, so I wet the net on the starboard side of the boat away from the fish. I wanted the net ready for action when it was time to act.

I quickly returned to Ace's side, whispering in his ear, "Very gently, see if you can ease the fish up so we can have a look at it. We've had it on for a long time, so at this stage you never know how well the hook is holding."

With great caution, Ace held the spool of his reel and pulled up slowly. The fish followed. He reeled in the line, dropping his rod tip as he did so, and eased the fish up another few feet.

Slowly the fish came into view. At first it was a blurry shape, like looking at a reflection in a distortion mirror. The closer it came to the surface the clearer the image became.

The salmon was huge. Even a few feet from the surface it was enormous. I turned to the helm and signalled for Sten to come down.

When he was standing beside me, he looked over the stern railing. "Jesus, we've got a live torpedo."

I peered out to get a better look at the fish. I swear, my stomach went cold. The lure was barely holding the fish by a small loop of flesh at the side of its mouth. The flesh had torn away, and if Ace dropped his rod tip the lure would disengage. Sten saw the situation at the same time; he spewed a short run of expletives. Ace had also seen the problem.

"Whatever you do," I said to Ace, "don't drop your rod tip and don't put any pressure on the fish. Stay in contact but in neutral contact." I sounded more excited than I'd intended. The whole group heard the excitement in my voice.

"What's up?" one of them asked.

"Sten, hand me the net," I said.

He was already on his way back with it. I was pleased I had taken the precaution of wetting it. This was going to be tricky.

I stepped even closer to Ace so I could speak softly but almost directly into his ear. "You saw how lightly it's hooked. We're going to get one chance at this. I want you to keep the fish close to the surface and lead it to me. I'll put the hoop in the water right in front of it and let it swim to the bottom of the basket. I'll lock it in, then Sten and I will pull it out. Rod tip up, then steer it to me. Got it?"

Ace nodded.

"Rod tip up and steer it to me," I repeated.

"Got it," Ace replied in an even voice. "How big do you think it is?"

"Over forty for sure, maybe sixty. Okay, lead it to me."

I put the hoop of the net in the water while still holding the bottom of the basket in my hand. To my horror I saw the lure flutter away from the fish's mouth. I looked over at Ace. He had involuntarily dropped his rod tip as I lowered the hoop of the landing net into the water. It was a sympathetic movement I'd seen before that released the pressure on the lure and allowed the hook to come free. I tried to force the hoop of the net around the salmon but it was gone with the flick of its tail, cruising disdainfully back to the depths of its ocean home.

The three of us were in total disbelief. Sten grabbed his head with his palms over his ears and repeated a single expletive a dozen times.

Ace looked at me, shaking his head. "What happened?"

It was not the right time to tell him he had just released his fish by allowing slack in the line. His group of friends had moved around us, peering overboard.

"Where the hell is the fish?" one of them demanded. "What happened?"

I did not have the heart to explain the details. I looked up to see Anna at the helm. She mimed the motion of dropping her rod tip. I nodded my head.

Meanwhile, Ace had reconstructed the last minutes of fishing and realized his mistake. "I dropped my rod tip, didn't I?" he asked. He was contorted with grief.

"It's the natural thing to do when the net goes into the water," I said. "It's called a sympathetic movement. I should have warned you. It's my fault."

Ace sat on the transom, burying his face in his hands. Joshua joined him and put his hand on his back, massaging him gently. "What would we do with a fish that big, buddy? They taste better when they're smaller."

Ace was inconsolable. He was weeping into his hands, punctuating his sobs with terse expletives.

I felt sick to my stomach. In the end, I always think it is my job to cover all probabilities and to get the fish into the boat. Sten, on the other hand, would be having distinctly different thoughts from mine. He would want to exercise the Cardinal on Ace's diminutive skull. He had the good sense to go below and allow the storm within him to work its way out. I could imagine him rolling his eyes to the skies and smacking a fist into the palm of his hand. I liked his intensity. In the meantime, however, I had to deal with Ace. He was still weeping tears of pain and loss with Joshua and his other friends in a semicircle around him.

I worked my way through the group surrounding Ace and sat on the transom beside him. "That was tough. It's always hard to lose a fish when you're sure it's about to go into the bottom of the basket. You played it perfectly right to the end. I should have warned you not to mimic my movements. Whichever way you slice it, that was a huge salmon. In all honesty I've never seen such a big one except in a few black and white pictures. It was a record of some sort, and you brought it to the net on fifteen-pound test line."

I wasn't sure if he was listening to me. He was weeping so loudly I had to raise my voice. When I looked up at his friends, there was little grief to be seen—most of them looked as though they were about to break out laughing. Quite honestly, I thought Ace was making heavy weather of an unfortunate situation. Again the thought struck me that something more was at stake. This loss meant more to Ace than simply losing a fish—in some way it was attached to his very sense of self. I felt sorry for him. It was, after all, just a fish.

"When we have a situation like this," I said, "the fisherman receives a certificate from us attesting to the size of the fish and the conditions under which it was lost." I was making it up as I spoke, trying to find some way of consoling him.

I looked at Sten, who had just returned to the aft deck. "Sten, without adding a pound and being ultra conservative, how big do you think that salmon was?"

"Over fifty pounds easy," he said without hesitating. "It could've gone over seventy but I would swear to fifty. If I'd seen it sideways it could have gone seventy. I wasn't sure the net would hold it. I was counting on gaffing it." He picked up the gaff with the plastic blue handle and yellow cap, which was on the deck at his feet. I believed every word he said. Sten was a wizard with weights. A large salmon like the one we'd just lost could very easily have swum through the net, ripping a hole in it. While the fish is still in the water, an expert with a gaff can drive the spike directly into the salmon's brain, killing it instantly and avoiding the battle of bringing it on board.

I lost no time in complementing Sten's efforts. "Ace, before disembarking, write your full name and address in the ship's guest book. I'll make out the certificate and Sten and I will sign it as witnesses. Then we'll send it to you. Is that okay with you?"

Ace had calmed down. His eyes were bloodshot; sitting slumped over on the transom, he looked emotionally exhausted. He was like a lost little boy who had just broken his favourite toy. There was little more we could do for him. I put my arm over his shoulder and gave him a squeeze.

"We have more than an hour of fishing left. I'll get you a fortified coffee, then we'll all get back to fishing. Its close relatives are waiting to be caught, and we know you have the lure that works."

I picked up his rod, cut off the lure and spun off the reel's wing nut to remove the spool. When I looked up, Sten was standing beside me with a fresh spool of line. As he handed it to me, we both smiled. We knew we had seen a fish of a lifetime and we had nearly landed it. For us it had been enough to see it in the water beside us with a net ready to scoop it on board. The fish was better off in the ocean, ready to forge its way up a river to spawn. We'd had the best of it, and now it was free. That was why we smiled.

I put the fresh spool of line on Ace's reel, tied on the lure and handed the rod back to him. "Back to work."

Ace smiled wanly as his friends broke into laughter. I went below to make a fresh pot of coffee.

With everyone at a fishing station and a hot cup of coffee beside them, I took a few minutes to sit at the dinette table and have a cup of tea. I had mixed emotions. I was just a little disappointed we had not landed our monster. My hope was that if the fish had been boated, Ace and his friends would have returned it to the ocean. But in reality I didn't think Ace could have given up such a salmon—it represented too much to him. In my heart I was pleased it had escaped and that it would find its natural ending. I hoped it would make its way up its river and spawn a new generation of giants. I finished my tea and went back on deck.

The Manly Crew was dispersed around the boat. Sten was at the wheel and Anna was fishing directly astern with Ace and Joshua on either side of her. A quiet conversation was taking place between the three of them. The other fishermen were talking among one another across the boat.

I felt a signal, that awareness bell of intuition I sometimes get. *Something's about to happen*, I thought. I looked up at Sten, who was facing away from the wheel. The *click, click, click* of the stylus marking an image on the paper sounder could be heard.

Sten pursed his lips and nodded his head. "Good feed down to fifty feet."

"Thirty pulls," I called out for everyone to hear. Immediately came the sound of line being stripped out another twenty feet. "First one to catch a fish has to eat a whole pumpkin pie," I announced.

The men made vomiting noises and derogatory remarks about pumpkin pie and its smell and colour. I was pleased they shared my opinion. "Okay, the next fisherman to catch a salmon gets a slice of my homemade peach pie," I added over their sound effects.

That induced a boisterous chorus of remarks. "That's better—now you're talking!" and some other more crude observations. Someone even led the group in "Three cheers for the peach pie." The mood turned light, and Ace joined in the three cheers. Sten was beaming; he was a real fan of my peach pie. He mimed cutting a huge slice of pie and eating it.

"We have to catch a fish first," I said to him.

He pointed over my head and gave two thumbs-up. I spun around to see Anna standing between Joshua and Ace with her wee rod doubled over. I looked back at Sten.

"Peach pie," he said.

Anna's reel screamed out line as Ace and Joshua reeled in their lines as fast as they could.

"Everyone but Ace and Joshua keep your lines in the water," I called out.

Anna was grinning as I approached her. The salmon was still tearing out line; her little rod was bent to the ferrule.

"Any size?" I asked. I could see by the bend of her rod that it was over twenty. "Do you think we should release this one?"

"Release your own fish," she said, still with a cheeky grin on her face.

"Would you like to hand it off?" I asked.

"We'll catch our own fish, thank you very much," an indignant Joshua shouted at me. "Leave the little girl alone. Let her play her fish." A chorus of disapproval arose from the Manly Crew. It made me smile.

"Come on, Anna," I said. "One of these fishermen would love to play your fish."

Anna hesitated. She knew we would sometimes hand off a fish we had hooked so guests could have the fishing experience.

"Don't listen to him. We'll catch our own fish," another outraged fisherman called out.

During this animated banter, Anna's salmon had taken a long first run, then stopped and thrashed on the surface in an attempt to throw the lure. Her rod was bouncing furiously. Her experience showed as she moved in synchronicity with the salmon. Never once did she lose contact with it nor did she ever put too much pressure on it. I hoped it wouldn't throw the lure.

I looked up at Sten, who was dancing in place and calling out instructions to Anna. He put up two fingers then one—twenty-one pounds. That would do just fine. I thought it might go twenty-five, but then I was her father.

It touched me how the Manly Crew got behind Anna and called out their support. They cheered her on when the salmon came rushing back at the boat and clapped when it sounded, taking out half the line in her spool. There was dead silence when we thought she had lost it and a huge roar when she made contact with it again and the reel started to sing. Sten's voice could be heard above the others shouting his support. The encouragement was so loud and consistent I was briefly reminded of a crowd of sports fans cheering on their team. In this case Anna was their team, but mingled into this were surely images of their own little girls at home.

Into the mix of this activity was my concern for Anna's sore arm and hand, still not recovered from the previous day. Now, twenty-four hours later, she was playing another strong fish. I had to ask. "How's your arm holding up?"

"It's sore," she replied without taking her eyes off the line in the water.

"Too sore to play your fish?"

"Forget it, Dad! Not you, not Sten. You are not gonna play my fish. Anyway, it's not mine yet." She was determined. She knew

I was concerned but she also knew both Sten and I would love to have a chance at her fish.

"If you need a break, there's no harm in asking us."

"Not a chance."

Someone from the Manly Crew shouted, "You tell him, girl."

Anna glanced up at me and we exchanged a smile. She knew how much I disliked that expression.

"I think this fish will go twenty-five pounds," one of the Manly Crew said to his friends. "I've got ten bucks that says it's twenty-five."

"You're on. I've got ten that says it's twenty-six."

They all called out their bets, and I had Sten go around the group and collect the money.

"What about the crew?" someone asked. "What does the crew think?"

I would not bet on Anna's fish, I told them, but asked Sten whether he wanted to throw ten dollars into the mix. I nodded at him as I said this, meaning I would cover his bet.

"I've got ten bucks on twenty-one pounds exactly," he said.

"You're in," Joshua called out. "Is everyone in who wants to be in?"

"I've got ten bucks on fourteen pounds." It was the voice of Ace.

"You've gotta be crazy," Joshua said, sounding irritated. "It's gotta go over twenty pounds, maybe even thirty."

"Mine went at least fifty," Ace said. "This one isn't a patch on mine." His tone was sharp and mean. He looked like a very small man. As a father I had an immediate surge of protectiveness, but I let it go. I realized Ace was still upset by his loss.

While the betting was going on behind Anna, she continued to focus on playing her fish. Slowly she brought it closer to the stern of the boat. She never allowed it any slack; she never eased up on the pressure. Despite her pain, I knew she would play it right to the net and that only when she was alone with Grandma would she complain about her arm.

Sten caught my attention and tapped the watch on his wrist. He held up two fingers and a zero. The fish was at our stern less than ten feet down. It was swimming backward and forward as though it was in a fish tank.

"What do you think, Anna? Do you think it's still green?" By that I meant not ripe, not ready to be netted. It's a standard fishing term.

"I don't know. It might be almost ready."

"I'm not sure."

On cue the salmon took a strong run, taking out fifty feet of line in a last effort to be free. Anna had almost anticipated this run. She knew the fish was now played out and it was time to net it.

I wet the net as Anna brought her salmon to the stern of the boat. Everyone peered at it as she brought it close to the surface in preparation for landing it. With the magnification of the water and their lack of experience, our Manly Crew collectively thought they had underestimated its size. As I swung it on board, loud clapping, whistling and hoots of pleasure ensued. Sten rang the ship's bell until we were nearly deaf. Even when I administered the *coup de grâce* with the Priest, they speculated it weighed in the mid-thirties, thumping Anna on the back and shaking her blistered hand. I gave her a hug and Sten came down from his position at the helm to shake her hand and weigh the fish.

My deluxe brass scales with the large porcelain dial told the truth.

"Twenty-one pounds exactly," Sten said, showing everyone the dial face on the scales. His tone was slightly smug and he wore an ear-to-ear grin. Not only was he pleased for Anna but he had won the bet. I knew never to bet against Sten when it came to the weight of a fish.

Impending darkness and a cool breeze ended the charter. Our Manly Crew walked down the dock with their bags of salmon, singing a song I had taught them. I could hear the faint refrain of "Oh, roll your leg over, Oh, roll your leg over . . ." as they made their way up the rattling metal ramp and into the parking lot.

Before they had disembarked, I asked Anna if she wanted to give her fish to our guests. Sometimes we did this if they had not caught anything. It was a hard question to ask her, and not really a fair one. Joshua had overheard my question and came to her rescue. He approached her with a large, fluffy dry fly held between his thumb and index finger. Slowly he reached up to her cap and hooked the pretty fly into it.

"I think you earned this today, and you earned keeping your fish. We have our own to take home."

It was a perfect end to the charter.

Their departure left the three of us alone on the boat. Anna's fish was already cleaned and bagged. The mugs, cutlery and plates were washed and the fishing gear was hosed down and stored. Anna's cap sported the large dry fly—she didn't want to part with it.

"Now, about that peach pie?" Sten said.

"Ten bucks a slice," I said. I was kidding, of course.

Without hesitation, he pulled out the wad of ten-dollar bills he had won and slapped one on the table. "It'll be worth every penny."

The three of us wolfed down the entire pie, which was meticulously divided into three. It was only as we started to eat that we realized we had not had dinner. We all agreed that homemade peach pie made a good dinner.

The following day was the big reveal. We put Anna's eighteen pounder and her twenty-one pounder on her grandparents' front lawn, then called Grandpa out to admire the brace of salmon she had caught. She seemed even more excited about showing off her catch to Grandpa than she had been when she caught them. That gave me enormous pleasure. I loved the relationship both my children had with their grandparents. Like all good relationships, it was never simple but so often satisfying.

Grandpa admired Anna's catch; he was thrilled for her. We got out the camera and took pictures, black and white photos that I still have. We even showed them off to the next-door neighbours as they walked by with their dog. They were impressed that a thirteen-year-old could play and land such big fish.

Grandpa put his arm around Anna and gave her a squeeze. "Oh, she can catch any size of fish. She can fish with the best of them, and she plays a mean hand of poker too."

That brought a laugh. After ogling the fish and hinting at how much they liked the tail section of a salmon, the neighbours continued on their way with their portly dachshund in tow.

"Which one shall I make into gravlax?" Grandpa asked.

We all loved gravlax, and we knew it was a lot of work to transform the salmon into that wonderful dish.

"The eighteen pounder," Anna said. "It's the perfect Grandpa size."

Glossary

An italicized word in a definition indicates that the word is also defined in this glossary.

action the spring or stiffness of a rod

amidships the middle of a boat

astern behind a boat

bag limit the maximum amount of fish a person may catch per day

bail a semi-circular piece of wire that guides the line around the spool of a reel

baitfish fish that the target species feed on; in the case of salmon, often herring or anchovies

ballast heavy material carried by a boat to provide stability

bilge   the bottom interior part of a boat

blank   the long, cylindrical part of a rod on which the grip, reel, line and guides are attached

boat hook   a long pole with a hook at one end used for retrieving things (or people) that fall overboard

bollard   a short, thick post on a dock around which mooring lines are secured

bow   the front of a boat

broadside   the side of a boat

bulkhead   the walls between compartments of a boat

Buzz Bomb   a registered trade name for a diamond-shaped lure

CB (Citizens Band)   a short-range form of radio communication used for chatting with other charter boats and fishermen

cleat   a fixture around which a rope is secured

companionway   stairs on a boat

compass bearing   the direction in which one is headed

crab pot   a circular trap used for catching crabs

crank   a unit of measurement equal to half a foot

deadhead a vertically submerged log

double ender a boat with a *bow* and *stern* of similar shape

downrigger equipment used to lower a fishing line, typically with a *flasher* and a lure or bait, to a specific depth. Single or multiple downriggers are mounted on the boat and each features a long steel cable with a lead ball at the end. A pressure clip holds the fishing line at the desired depth, but allows the line to come free when a fish strikes. *See Figures 1–3*

drag the part of a reel that lets line out when a fish runs

drift fishing fishing while drifting in the current with the boat's engine off

dry fly an artificial fly used in fly fishing

feed fish that the target species feed on; in the case of salmon, often herring or anchovies

Fig. 1 DOWNRIGGER SETUP

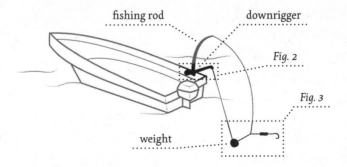

Fig. 2   DOWNRIGGER EQUIPMENT

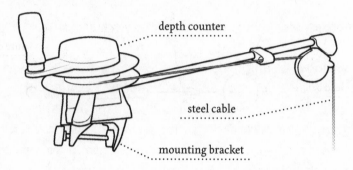

ferrule   a ring on a fishing rod that guides the line

flashers   long, thin pieces of shiny metal that rotate to attract a fish's attention. *See Figure 3*

float   a buoyant object that is attached to a line and used to suspend bait at a certain depth

freeboard   the distance between the waterline and the deck of a boat

gaff   *n.* a pole with a hook at the end used for killing fish; *v.* to use this tool on a fish

galley   the kitchen area on a boat

gillie   a local fishing guide

goose   to give the engine a shot of energy, similar to stepping on the accelerator in a car

Fig. 3 LURE AND FLASHER ASSEMBLY

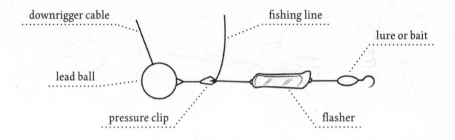

green describes a fish not ready to be netted

grilse a young Atlantic salmon returning to freshwater for the first time

groundswell a strong swelling of the sea caused by a storm or gale

head the bathroom on a boat

helm the steering wheel of a boat

jig *n.* a type of lure with more than one hook; *v.* to fish using this lure

keel the bottom of a boat

leader a short length of line or wire that attaches a fishing line to a hook

lee   shelter

make way   to be propelled through the water by oar, engine or sail

on loose lines   describes a vessel that is attached to a dock with slack lines

periscope depth   just above the surface of the water

pilot   the skipper of a boat

plane   to move a boat quickly enough for the *bow* to lift out of the water

plug   a type of lure made of wood or plastic

port   the left side of a boat, when facing forward

presentation   the appearance of a lure, including the size, shape, colour, motion through the water, etc.

pull   a unit of measurement equal to about two feet

run   a migration of salmon from the ocean up a river in order to spawn

shoal   a group of fish

shoe of the keel   material (often wood) attached to the base of a *keel* to protect it

single-action reel   a reel without gears or *bail*

slack tide   the period of time between the reversal of tidal currents

slip   a docking area

slip lines   to unfasten the lines that tie a boat to a dock

slug   a large fish

smolt   a young salmon

spinner   a type of lure that spins as it moves through the water

spinning reel   a reel featuring an open-faced spool and a *bail*

split cane   a handmade rod made from lengths of bamboo that are glued together

spoon   a type of lure that looks like a tablespoon

stanchion   an upright pole or support on a boat

starboard   the right side of a boat, when facing forward

stern   the back of a boat

strike   to bite a hook; to yank up a rod to set the hook in a fish's mouth

strip out line   pull out line

sulker   a fish that doesn't want to run or make its way to the surface

synched   tightened or held fast

take the strain   to slowly put the tension on a tow rope

test   the tensile strength of a line; the amount of stress it can take before it snaps

tidal line   the convergence point of two tidal currents

transom   the back of a boat

treble hook   a three-pronged hook

trolling   fishing while a boat is in motion

V-drive   a propulsion system used in boats

vent area   the anus of a fish

VHF (Very High Frequency)   a long-range form of radio communication used for rescue work, making telephone calls and contacting marinas and harbour masters

Acknowledgments

I would like to thank the staff at Harbour Publishing for their understanding and humour. Special thanks to Arlene Prunkl for her editing skills and soft approach. *Slàinte*, to all of you!

33 Japanese